# Coming Home

# Coming Home

## A Spiritual Memoir

## Lori Vos

SHANTI ARTS PUBLISHING
BRUNSWICK, MAINE

# Coming Home: A Spiritual Memoir

Published by Shanti Arts Publishing
Cover and interior design by Shanti Arts Designs

Cover image by Raymond Vos and used with his permission.

Shanti Arts LLC
Brunswick, Maine
www.shantiarts.com

Printed in the United States of America

Scripture quotations marked (ESV) are from the ESV® Bible (The Holy Bible, English Standard Version®), copyright © 2001 by Crossway, a publishing ministry of Good News Publishers. Used by permission. All rights reserved. The ESV text may not be quoted in any publication made available to the public by a Creative Commons license. The ESV may not be translated into any other language.

Scripture quotations marked (NIV) are taken from the Holy Bible, New International Version®, NIV®. Copyright © 1973, 1978, 1984, 2011 by Biblica, Inc.™ Used by permission of Zondervan. All rights reserved worldwide. www.zondervan.comThe "NIV" and "New International Version" are trademarks registered in the United States Patent and Trademark Office by Biblica, Inc.™

Scripture quotations marked (NRSV) are from the New Revised Standard Version Bible, copyright © 1989 National Council of the Churches of Christ in the United States of America. Used by permission. All rights reserved worldwide.

This book is a memoir, written from the author's recollections of experiences that occurred over many years. The dialogue presented in this book is not intended to represent word-for-word transcripts; events and scenes are not precise representations. The names and characteristics of some individuals have been changed to protect privacy. In all cases, the author has remained true to the feeling and meaning of what happened and what was said.

ISBN: 978-1-956056-50-1 (softcover)
ISBN: 978-1-956056-51-8 (ebook)

Library of Congress Control Number: 2022943941

*for Ray and for Marianne,*
*and for sheep outside the fold everywhere*

# Contents

# Acknowledgments

Thank you to my editor and publisher, Christine Cote, for birthing this book so beautifully.

Thank you to all who, with open hearts and discerning minds, read and responded to early drafts: to my writing partner, Maureen Garvie; to the Stillpoint writing group—Susan Mockler, Rebecca Gowan, and Jane Russell Corbett; and to Megan Webster, Julie Sigrist, Nikki Sigrist, and Liz Parsons.

Thank you to those who have walked this journey with me for a season or for a lifetime, companions too numerous to list here. I am unspeakably grateful to you all, but especially to my husband Raymond Vos and my sister Marianne Kond. My tribute to them exists in these pages.

And to the One who has sheltered, guided, and mended me, I say with full heart: "Great is your faithfulness, Lord, unto me."

# Introduction

THE FORM THIS BOOK TAKES MAY BE UNUSUAL FOR SOME. It began as a series of personal essays about the most redemptive aspects of my life: the places I've lived; the home I've shared with my husband; the significant relationships I've had with friends, surrogate mothers, and communities. But as a dear friend pointed out, these healing streams are only half of my life story. "Redemption doesn't fully make sense," she said, "unless we know what you have been redeemed from." So I understood that it was important to relate the painful, sometimes horrific details of my childhood experiences and the stages of leaving my family behind to give the reader a complete picture of my healing history. The direct narrative passages have no titles; they take the reader chronologically through my life and serve as bridges between the essays. I have included poems as another way to experience the story, as a glimpse into a moment, a feeling, or an insight connected to a theme in one of the longer pieces.

Some of the narrative passages will be difficult to read. My friend Claire, an early reader of this book, knew what was coming, and she needed to be reassured that I was all right. "Are you okay now?" she asked. "Are you well? If I know you're all right, I can make it through the hard parts." I could reassure her that I am very well. My prayer now is that this book will convey, to her and to others, the hope that comes when darkness, even deep darkness, is ultimately overcome by the light.

My life has been fueled and shaped by two primary impulses. My need to know where God was during the worst moments of my childhood has sent me deep into the wilderness of my past and far from the certainties of religion. I have hoped to discover the reality of a loving God beneath my dark foundation of injury, and I hoped to find that the presence of God within and without was more significant in my childhood than the damaging influence of my parents. Otherwise, the idea of God was meaningless to me, and I was alone in the world to make of my fractured life whatever I could.

The second impulse has lain quietly but insistently beneath my often compulsive busyness and striving: the longing for rest. This passage from the biblical book of Matthew has long held out hope for me: "Come to me, all you who are weary and burdened, and I will give you rest. Take my yoke upon you and learn from me, for I am gentle and humble in heart, and you will find rest for your souls. For my yoke is easy and my burden is light." (Matt. 11:28–30, NIV) Rest for me means a sense of peace that can permeate and hold my inmost self in the storms of circumstance and feeling.

But deeper than my desire for rest has been my longing for home, for a place in my inmost self where I am safe and held in loving arms. A place where I know beyond thought but deep in my bones that everything was, is, and will be all right. All is well. The need to find God was birthed in the desperation and homelessness of my childhood; the longing for rest and home was a gift. Both have carried me into ever deeper relationship with God and with myself.

I am a child of my parents, so my story begins with theirs. Because they died young, my father at forty-one and my mother at sixty-seven, and I was estranged from my mother for ten years before her death, I learned little about their pasts directly from them. Maybe the understanding many of us have of our parents is dim and impressionistic. What have been left to me are swatches of memories from old photos, family stories, and my own sketchy recollections.

From my father's sisters, one older and one younger than my father, I have only small snippets of information about him. I know he loved music and had a guitar propped in a corner of his room in the old farmhouse where he spent several of his teenage years.

The house belonged to the fruit farm in Niagara that his parents eventually bought after emigrating from Estonia. Both of my aunts, currently in their eighties, will now talk a bit about life in Estonia, about the family's escape in 1944 as the Russians advanced into the country, and about their years in Sweden as refugees. They like to relate stories of their early years in Canada when they distinguished themselves as students in high school and university. They were accomplished women in the 1950s, a time when it was unusual for even non-immigrant women to attain a college education. They also talk of a hard-working life on the farm, of the times as young women when they drove the family truck to the cities of Hamilton and Owen Sound to sell peaches door-to-door. But they are generally disinclined to talk about their brother, the teenager who escaped the austerity of farm life by drinking hard with his high school buddies and sometimes not returning home at night. I know something of him from this time in his life from an old photo. He is standing proudly, slim and strong in jeans and white t-shirt, his foot propped on the bumper of his navy Chrysler Plymouth, bearing an astonishing resemblance to a young James Dean. Smart and athletic, he nevertheless struggled to fit in in high school as he tried to learn a new language and culture. He was vulnerable to the destructive ways of the group who finally accepted him, including two older Latvian boys and my younger mother. They urged him to join the real world instead of going to university like his sisters. He became the family disappointment, later the family shame, and finally the family tragedy as he moved from high school to jobs in the automotive industry, married young and later destroyed his family life, and finally took his own.

According to my uncle, my mother's eldest brother, my mother was a wild child from the start, often willfully plunking herself down in the middle of the road during snowy walks to school, refusing to budge, frustrating her helpless siblings. Her propensity to control others through her tantrums continued well into her adult life, an effective means of survival. Beyond her stubbornness, in high school she was intelligent enough to sometimes do her older sister's homework besides her own and would have studied to become a teacher if circumstances had allowed. Like my father, she was athletic and musically gifted; she had a beautiful singing voice. Like his, her family had struggled, hers escaping the Depression years in rural Saskatchewan for an almost equally poverty-stricken life in Ontario. My mother's mother had had her first child at sixteen;

three more followed. By the time her children were teenagers, my tempestuous grandmother's life with my gentle grandfather, a life that was stormy for years perhaps because of her drinking problem, fell apart. She fled alone to relatives in Massachusetts, leaving her family behind.

My troubled parents found each other in high school, then married at nineteen and twenty years old. In my mind, my father was leaving a stern farm life and a matriarchal immigrant family; my mother was looking for a lifeline as her family disintegrated. But beyond these circumstances was the one that set them permanently on the wrong track. While they were both still teenagers, my newly pregnant mother told my father she would seek an abortion only if he married her. Panicked, he fled the mess of his life for the big city. But his father convinced him to return. I remember a photo of my parents' wedding day, my father finely handsome in his white suit, and my mother uncharacteristically demure with her wide smile and unruly light brown curls tamed. She and her maid of honor are seated; behind them my mother's brothers, looking grim and immovable as guards, are flanking my father.

She used to tell me she knew she had made a mistake the evening of their wedding day. During what should have been an intimate time, my father went out and left her, likely for the hotel bar, returning inebriated hours later. He may have realized his mistake too. But they tried in the early years to make their union work. According to my mother, they moved away from their families to Stratford, a charming small Ontario town where my father had found a good job and my mother took pride in setting up their home. Several years later, they moved back to the region of their families because my father had accepted a better position, this time at an automotive parts manufacturing plant. Always highly proficient at math, he was able to do the work of an engineer despite his lack of education. They bought a white-sided, black-shuttered bungalow in a nice neighborhood and settled in.

Seven years after they married, my mother became pregnant. That my father was furious with her, violently tried to cause a miscarriage, tells me that he may have been tricked by my mother into producing a child he didn't want: me. He may always have known he was unfit for fatherhood. I suspect my parents' lives continued to be troubled, and starting a family was my mother's way of trying to save a failing marriage. Two intelligent, conflicted young people trapped in a domestic life that was limited and unhappy for both of them now faced parenthood. Even the sense I've tried to make of their histories, even the rage and willfulness that grew in them from their early years can't explain what they came to do to their children, to me.

And so my story begins.

# PART ONE

# Place: The Beginning

M Y MOTHER AND I BOTH USED MENTAL TRICKS TO protect ourselves from the truth. She changed the story; I forgot it completely. The process of healing for me began with remembering.

My dark history started sometime after my sister's birth and before my third birthday. I can pinpoint the time because in my thirties I discovered a photograph of myself on that third birthday wearing a new navy dress with white flowers across the front that suited my white-blond hair. I wondered, when I studied this photo, at the small marks on both of my shins. At first I thought they were mosquito bites, but then I realized it was March, not mosquito season. The marks were bruises from my father's fingertips pressing into my flesh as he pulled my little legs apart.

He came in the night into the room I shared with my infant sister, yanked the covers from my bed, and fumbled off my pajama bottoms. Then he split me in two. When he finished, he wiped himself clean on my pajama top and stumbled out of the room. When the door shut behind him, the night became black, black, so much blacker than it had been moments before.

My mother used to tell me, when I was older, that as a child I had had tonsillitis so badly she would come into my room sometimes in the morning and find blood all over my pajama front. I didn't think to question this story, though I didn't remember having terrible sore throats, and I still had my tonsils.

The morning after my father first hurt me, my mother found

me in a mess in my bed. She exploded with rage, not at my father but at me. So I lost both parents at once, and though I continued to live in a house with a family, my state of homelessness began as I retreated inside myself. And I became lost to my parents as a daughter, serving instead as a scapegoat to help them cope with the terrible entrapment of their marriage.

For the next two-and-a-half years, my father continued his drunken visits to my room on Friday nights while my mother continued to blame me for his actions. The mornings afterward, her treatment of me grew increasingly bizarre. While I was in the bathtub, she began to make shallow, crisscrossing cuts in my thighs or the fleshy parts of my hands with a razor blade "to let the pain out." Then, when I was four years old, she conducted a late night ritual that suggests to me now she went outside our home for help. It seems possible that someone pointed her to a higher power, a diabolical rather than a benevolent one; she found someone who taught her how to access that power. The night of the ritual, the mother I knew seemed to have vacated the body of the woman standing robed in black at the foot of my bed. After instructing my father to place a small knife inside of me, she began chanting in a gravelly voice words that were incomprehensible to me. I lay stunned and mesmerized by the glowing yellow eyes locked onto mine. When the chant was over and the knife removed, she told me in her own voice that I had just been punished and that God couldn't love little girls like me.

Through these years I learned to cope, as children do. There were hours and days of ordinariness that gave me respite, small pleasures to cling to. Regular walks to the Bookmobile, a small bus loaded with books that we could choose from and bring home. Curious George books were my favorites, with their bright covers and stories our mother would read of a spunky mischievous monkey who was always getting away but always being found by the man in the yellow hat who loved him. I also tried to take care of my sister in whatever fumbling ways I could. We would sit together on the thick ocher carpeting of our living room, and I would show her how to make small towers of wooden blocks, pointing out the letters on the blocks' shiny red and white faces. I would carefully place one block on top of another and then give her one to try with. She would attempt to grasp the block in her chubby little fist but couldn't hold it well enough to put it down deliberately, so she would fling it from her hand instead. Two sisters, absorbed in the play-world of our living room or immersed in the worlds of books that took us from our own.

I also tried to please my mother by becoming highly sensitive to her needs and wishes and doing my best to help her. I made sure I cleaned up our toys and set the table for dinner each night, thinking that my good behavior might prevent or lessen the pain and terror I knew was coming. In the nightmare of this childhood, I lost myself, lost consciousness of the damage I was sustaining as fear replaced love in my body and psyche. As despair drained away any feeling that I was good and the world was a good place in which to be. And so I lost a sense of home with myself, with others, and with God.

Throughout her life, my mother never acknowledged her behavior during those dark years of our lives, nor did she ever admit knowing about my father's abuse of me. She too may have lost consciousness, or chosen to forget, the worst. What she was always honest about, though, was my father's alcoholism; she described us all as victims of his problem. From time to time she would tell of my coming to her one day when I was close to five years old and asking, "Why do we have to live this way?" and her response, "Because your father is sick." Then she would say that I replied, "Yes, but why do we have to live this way?" As she related it, this was the moment she decided to leave my father.

I don't recall this childhood conversation, so I can't say for sure that it happened. What I do know is that at the time I was nearing my fifth birthday, I felt myself beginning to slip away. I was sliding into a fog between consciousness and unconsciousness, and my body felt as fragile as a dragonfly's wing. I believe now that my mother saw the state I was in and suddenly realized there could be consequences of continuing in our situation that she wasn't prepared to face. So she left my father and took my sister and me across the city to a new house and a new life. Though the move forward was lurching—she spent six months in a psychiatric hospital and my father came to live with us for a while—eventually she came home and soon afterward he left for good. The three of us settled into our new life in a quiet, treed old neighborhood—once a village on its own—just two blocks from the lake. For me, hope rose on the horizon like the merest lifting of darkness by the light of dawn.

# The Village at Lakeside

I am at the beach, sitting on a large rock at the shoreline. The old willow shading me has been dropping fuzzy brown corkscrews. Their sharp, woodsy smell drifts on the breeze and fills my nostrils with the memory of Grandma and Grandpa's cottage several miles west along the old Lakeshore Road. The water is clearer now than when I was a child; I can see through the shallows the regular ridges of soft sand, tufts of seaweed floating above, veins of light shimmering and shifting with the incoming waves. Ducks are playing on the surface of the lake, squawking and flapping at each other. Sometimes a graceful pair glides by, the male's head a brilliant bottle green.

And always there is the plashing, gulping sound of water hitting stone, the rhythmic shush of waves fanning along the sand where the rocks end and the beach begins. The sound of the waves was the music of my childhood, the lake wind its breath. My sight was formed by the vast stretch of the horizon, the limitless vault of blue above it. That open horizon gave me an aching for eternity. Here at the shore I learned to look, to discover in the beauty and solitude a presence, immutable as the great lake itself, watching, listening, waiting.

My sister's house is the place I stay when I return to the village. In the mornings, I hear the back door slam and the van's engine hum as she and her partner leave for work. Then I am alone. Sometimes I lie reading in bed, enjoying a silence broken only by the chatter of birds or the sound of a passing car. Sometimes I look out the window at branches and blue sky that make me feel I am living in the treetops.

I dress and pad downstairs, out to the backyard. It is mid-May; the new spring growth is a pretty promise of the coming Niagara lushness. The Japanese pear is white with blossoms that send a peculiar pungency into the air. Around the perimeter of the yard, a gray wooden fence supports climbing hydrangea behind beds of violets, bleeding hearts, and forget-me-nots. I stand on the deck and gaze down at tender green blades of grass, hesitant to crush them with my feet.

I turn and pick my way over the pebbled driveway to the front of the house. As I lift my head and look before me, I feel my chest expand with the openness of the view. I am standing at the top of a steep embankment that leads to the edge of the river, a wide river that wears its history in various scenes. To my left is the old red brick factory, a former mill; near it the stone locks that used to open to the canal and the great lake beyond. Now the heavy gates are still, aside from the water that rushes over them. Over the water, a new bridge curves up toward the city. But the river is unconstrained in front of me by fetters of stone and cement; it is a wide, flat stretch of silver. Today it is gently sparkling in the sunlight, its surface lined occasionally by geese trailing their webbed feet as they land. I let my gaze rest in the stillness. Then I look right and up the rowing course, where buoys bob in the waves, to the distant island with its boathouse and sweeping willows. Not many rowers are on the course, just a few scullers steadily dipping and pulling their oars. I inhale the freshness, the peace. This simple waterscape seems so vulnerable, gives up its beauty so quietly, asking nothing from me but to receive what I can in that moment.

As I walk the wide streets of the village, I visit trees as old friends. One stands at the curve in the road where Ann Street turns into Bayview Avenue. I sit on the bench beside the tree and look out over the water. Here the shoreline rises in a sharp slope to the street; there are no houses, so the view is broad, open. This tree sees far, knows the moods of the lake, silently watches the comings and goings of those who cross its surface. I watch with it as the lake shifts and rolls, blue gray, under the weight of a lowering sky.

I move from the tree and the view and walk several blocks along Dalhousie Avenue. As a child, I couldn't identify these trees, apart from the familiar maples; now I know there is chestnut and oak, fir and spruce, the occasional willow, and some I still can't name. I knew and still know these trees as towering giants whose leaves are so high above me I can barely make out their shapes except when they shed them in autumn. They are all wide trunks and thick branches reaching up to splay and leaf, meeting over the shaded streets below. Where sunlight falls through this canopy it brightens lawns, houses, and sidewalks with soft, moving patches of illumination.

I reach what used to be the Jowetts' house and the biggest tree in the village. I tell people that its trunk is so huge I can't put my arms halfway around it. I look at that great trunk now, its ridges and thick ropes of gray bark, the way its roots pool at its base before submerging in the earth. I step up onto a ledge of root and stretch my arms around the tree, hoping no one will drive or walk by and see me. As I stand there, fingers locked in grooves of rough skin, I am warmed by the light this tree has absorbed, soothed by the strength that rises from deep roots to new branches smaller than my fingertips.

Nearby, around two street corners, I reach the tall straight maple that shades my childhood home. The rounded shelves of the tree's roots were just right to stand or sit on when I was small. They are still just right. As I step up and lean my body against the trunk, I think about what this tree has seen. Many years ago, it watched a woman and two small pajama-clad girls run from a man too drunk to catch them, run three blocks to a phone booth on the village's main street. This tree is a guardian in ways my understanding can only begin to touch. It stands strong, swayed by wind and rain but firmly rooted, seeing through windows and into yards, absorbing sorrow like sunlight. I am grateful; I know it stood guard over me.

When I grew up here, Port, as the village was called, was rough. Then, as now, the hotel bars were dingy, giving off a sour, acrid smell of smoke, stale beer, and urine: reminders of Port's past as a canal and shipbuilding town with its transient workers and sailors frequenting the local grog shops.

At McArthur, the local public school, some of the kids were like me—poor, from broken homes. And not like me—many were already hard and hopeless. Still, the school was a good home. Built in the late nineteenth century, it was a tall red-brick building with a bell tower and narrow windows that reached to the top of high-ceilinged classrooms. Inside, there was dark wood everywhere—staircases, banisters, doors, baseboards, and floors that creaked under our feet as we made our way to our rooms and desks every morning.

I remember every classroom, each past configuration of desks, doors, chalkboards, and windows, and I remember my teachers. Mrs. Thomas was my favorite. Slight, sprightly, middle-aged, with a head of chestnut curls and bright hazel eyes, she moved quickly and saw everything. I was fortunate to have her as my teacher in grades five and six. Like all good teachers, she tried to push us to our best, made learning an adventure. She saw me in ways I had never been seen before, a recognition that gave me hope.

McArthur School is gone now, demolished quietly and without

question more than a decade ago. I saw it for the last time the day before it was reduced to a pile of splintered wood and broken bricks. A former owner of my sister's home salvaged the piece of the belltower that reads 1877–1977. It sits on her front lawn and reminds us of the stories, faces, and classrooms, the new worlds and new selves, that still flow through our veins.

More than the school will be demolished soon. Most of the old buildings lining Lock Street and Lakeport Road will be razed by a developer's will, deep pocketbook, and heavy machinery. The rough edges of Port will be gone. The two lighthouses that have stood watch on the far pier for over a century will be dwarfed by a towering condominium, a beacon of progress and commerce. Will the carefully coiffed, high-heeled shoppers of the future feel the ghostly disdain of the towmen and canal laborers of the past?

This time, the destruction won't come without protest. The voice of the community, seeking to preserve its heritage, has been strong. But the judge who heard the case saw only the promise of new business; Goliath stood firm against the sharp sting of David's stones. Now the village stands at the cusp of another shift in its history, uneasy with its coming identity, its new, imposed face.

As I walk the quiet midday streets, I slow as I reach the old captain's house at the corner of Dalhousie and Ann. A two-story, square wooden structure, painted white and green, it sits solidly on its corner lot, as stalwart as I imagine a ship's captain would have been. I come to this place in my daydreams. When I am troubled or anxious, I return to this spot in my mind and it always looks as it does now—dressed in the garb of spring. Before the square front windows, the magnolia drops its petals. Tulips and daffodils are dabs of bright color bordering the lawn.

What is it about this place that draws me when I am far away? I stand and breathe the lake wind, feel it toss my hair against my face. I watch sunlight play across the grass and touch the heads of flowers. Immovable, the house stands against time, its only shifting shapes the glinting reflections in its windows.

I have never lived in this house or on the streets that border it, but here I am home. I stand at the corner, the site of the old school behind me, the lake visible on the horizon ahead. My feet have grown roots that have cracked the sidewalk, thrust deep into the earth. This soil, this house, these trees, this lake, this body, these eyes, this life. This life.

# Great Lake

As I ride the rails again, from the big city back home,
I thrill to it: a glimpse of that immense presence, the lapis strip
widening as we near the shore, at times buffed by pale light
to a silver sheen, at times rocking a star-pricked path.

Today a little girl across the aisle points out the window and shouts
*my lake. My lake.* I follow her finger to the band of blue glittering
in the sun and smile at her fierce possessing: it is my lake, too.

When I was a child the lake lay north, flat beneath the high sweep
of sky, its stillness the only steadiness I knew amid shape-shifters,
sand-face features twisted by wind, voices like gulls' cries
shrieking too close and wheeling away.

In the town I live now
the lake is south.
There the horizon heaps
with dots and dashes,
the Morse code of islands.
No openness to open to.

But now on this train, and ahead to that fettered horizon,
the lake waits for me. Together we are without guile or striving, at rest.
It sits shimmering in its bounds of rock and sand; I sit beholding it,
in body or mind's eye—
holding open a place within where that vast stillness lies.

# PART TWO

# School Years

HEN I THINK ABOUT MY EARLY YEARS AT SCHOOL, I'm struck by the clarity and vividness of my memories. I can see the turquoise blue of the sleeping mat belonging to the boy who was allowed extended naps during kindergarten. The disapproval in the delicate features of my grade two teacher when a boy kissed the bump on my forehead that came from a fall during recess. The patch of asphalt at the end of the schoolyard slide of ice that caused the fall. I remember all of my teachers' and most of my classmates' names and the location of my desk in each high-ceilinged room of the old school.

In contrast to my memories of school, I think of my home at this time as dark and shadowed. In my mind, my mother and sister, and the middle-aged Englishwoman next door who sometimes looked after us, seem insubstantial. I know that my sister went to nursery school and my mother attended night classes, later finding work as a bookkeeper. My father became peripheral, present only during Sunday visits with my sister and me. Along with the presence of these shadowy figures, my home was always dense with dread, with the knowledge that my mother's struggles could turn her into the terrible someone I had seen as a younger child.

Ever vigilant, I watched her moods shift from the fun-loving, creative highs of good days to the tearful or angry storms of bad ones. On good days, after dinner she would crank up the volume on the radio and we three would dance around the kitchen, snapping our dishtowels at each other in time to the pop tunes filling the air. Or have a big, farmer's style breakfast, with bacon, eggs, and fried potatoes, in the sunlit warmth of a late Saturday morning after we finished our chores. But even on good days, part of me knew to stay detached, to try to prepare myself for the worst. But the worst was unimaginable, and it came out of nowhere. The autumn I was seven years old, late on Hallowe'en night, my mother dragged me from sleep and from my room toward our bathroom. I didn't know what was going to happen, but my body switched into high alert, waves of panic pulsing through my limbs. In the room, two black-robed figures were waiting, their shadows moving up and down the wall in the flickering candlelight. Again a knife was thrust inside me, but this time I was in a bathtub, numb as I watched my blood turning the water pink. Then I was led downstairs into the basement—more blood with its rusty smell, but not mine. The slippery, warm feeling of the guts my face was shoved into, causing vomit to rise in my throat. The next day, my sister grew distressed when the family cat did not come home.

Five months later, there was a final ritual, but worse than the last, in our secluded back yard at night. A ring of black figures, their hoods shading their faces from candlelight. My mother among them, watching as my sister and I were drawn into the circle to witness the sacrifice, this time an infant. Killed by the ringleader with a knife to its heart. After the death, as two figures took the little body and disappeared behind dense evergreens at the back of the yard, the leader pulled me aside. He ordered me to the ground and raped me, the still-wet ceremonial knife lying near my head. But what was happening in my body couldn't touch the horror of watching my small sister being led by two others into our old shed. After I was released and she emerged, we crept away from the group through the cold dew back to our house and our bedroom, where I spent the rest of the night huddled on the floor between my bed and the wall. It was the night of Good Friday, the time of the death of innocents, of innocence.

The next morning, I awoke to find myself back in my bed with my mother at the foot, shaking me.

"Get up!" she barked, irritated with me. I looked up at her, not able to will my arms and legs to move, for the first time not able to scramble to obey.

"You're not sick, for heaven's sake. Get up and get going. You have chores to do."

She shook me again, then stood back as I rolled to my side, threw back the covers, and hauled myself out of bed. A look of satisfaction crossed her face. This is what my mother taught me: no matter what happened, never acknowledge it between us or to anyone else, and above all, keep going. Don't be sick, don't be weak, just keep going.

As my aunt let slip much later, soon after these instances my mother's new boyfriend found her stash of dark paraphernalia—the robes, the black candles—and trashed it all. The worst was over. But I was floundering. The horror of recent experiences and now the presence of my mother's boyfriend—a stocky, heavy-drinking Englishman who lived with us in the months he wasn't away at a construction site—left me feeling profoundly dislocated, homeless. One gray spring late afternoon, desperate for comfort and connection, I asked for a ride to my best friend's house so I could go to her birthday party. As my mother's boyfriend parked his rattley station wagon in front of her house, he remarked that no one seemed to be home. I said that the house was dark because the party was supposed to be a surprise for my friend. Satisfied, he drove off. But when no one came to answer my knock on the door, I had nowhere to go. I had no choice but to trudge all the way back home in the chill and now dark evening, to confess, and to hear the snap of my mother's belt as it split the air and cut into the backs of my legs. I never lied to her again, nor did I, after that day, ever try to escape my home and seek comfort in another.

Through grades three and four, as I tried to carry on with the activities of school and home, I found myself in another fog, with even my physical eyesight diminishing. A coldness had settled into the core of my being, and the loneliness I felt at home extended to school, where I could no longer connect with either teachers or classmates. I simply fumbled along as best I could in those dim years until grade five began and I was delivered into a place of color, and clarity, and care. A place of hope.

# A Cloud of Mothers

*Since we are surrounded by so great a cloud of witnesses... let us run with perseverance the race that is set before us.*

—Hebrews 12:1 (ESV)

I have always considered myself an orphan in light of growing up with deeply troubled parents. My mother was particularly dangerous. I learned early not to need her, not to steal behind her, wrap my arms around her waist and lay my head against her warm back. I learned to store, deep, deep, the knowledge that at any moment she could turn on me in rage. Connected to her by fear, I tried to appease and escape her at the same time, tried always to be good enough to prevent her wrath. With that sole focus, I lived in a fog of disconnection from myself, unaware of my body, my needs, and my feelings, devoid of dreams or hopes for my future.

What did I need to awaken to myself and begin living in my body? I needed witnesses—witnesses who could see and reflect to me a self that existed apart from my mother.

Mora Thomas brought the vibrant color of Oz to my barren Kansas. After years of fearful vigilance and dull hopelessness at home, when I was ten years old my spirit began to stir in response to the life in her classroom.

She wasn't the soft, plump, warm-voiced kind of woman one would expect in a mother figure. Mrs. Thomas was short and energetic, with bright eyes and quick movements that showed she meant business. But she wasn't harsh; she was simply present, in a crackling, electric way. I see her vividly in her blue plaid polyester suit and neon pink scarf, with her curly brown hair and large-framed glasses that made her round face owly. And I hear her voice, nasal and sharp-edged but full of inflection as she read to us.

She read to us every day. And as the verses and tales rolled on and under and through me, I was carried on a current much more invigorating than sympathy. Passages from the Bible, long sections of *The Hobbit*, and tales by Farley Mowat awakened my courage and strengthened my battered psyche. The characters who often inhabited strange or magical lands, who faced terrible evils, walked with trembling but determined steps through adversity to the brightness beyond. They gave me hope.

It has been over forty years since I sat in her grade five/six classroom, but in my mind I can readily slip into my place there. The room felt safe. Our desks were in groups, facing inward—a friendlier arrangement than long, stark rows. Tall windows let in abundant light every afternoon. Warm and pleasant, the classroom was full of color, activity, and fascinating information. In social studies, we learned about roses in Bulgaria and the empty Australian outback. At each week's end we played math baseball with a ferocious intensity. And beyond the subject matter were her small gestures of recognition that made me happy: the smiley faces she sometimes drew on my math tests or the chance to read a thrilling passage aloud to the class.

One bright day in late spring, she asked me to stay inside after the last bell rang and the other students went home. She wanted me to clean blackboards and chalk brushes with her. I don't know why she chose that day; maybe she noticed something about me that concerned her. I don't remember what we talked about while we drew brushes across the blackboards in big, sweeping strokes and then went out into the warm spring air to bang them against the side of the school. I don't think we talked much at all, but I do remember the white rectangles of chalk stamped on the red bricks and the feeling of being special to someone.

She must have known somehow that I was in trouble, though she never asked any questions about my life at home. She kept a professional distance. But it felt to me like a watchful distance; she saw me. And her positive regard affirmed my being, affirmed that my presence in the world was good. That loving stance began to turn the blighted, withering landscape of my young life into a greening place. A place where, one day, joy could start to grow.

Shirley Sax was the bravest person I came to know. Early in our years together, when as a teenager I worked in her gift shop, I watched her standing precariously on a chair, reaching to place a doll up on a high shelf. I was young and uncertain; I didn't know enough to take the task from her and insist she rest. She was shaky from the effects of MS, a disease that had already plagued her for about ten years by then.

She had also survived a painful, acrimonious divorce and the raising of her three sons alone. Her struggles had forged and refined in her an incredible force of will. She had a fierce resistance to giving up even when her body was failing. A determination to cling to a positive outlook in the grimmest circumstances, to have faith in goodness in the face of betrayal.

She was often stubborn, but loveliness in many forms had already softened the contours of her life and character. In her person she was lovely, with her thick, wavy hair and the smattering of freckles across her nose. She was small but pleasingly rounded and always gracefully dressed. As she worked in the gift shop, her hands seemed so sensitive to the beautiful things she unpacked and arranged with deftness and care.

And I saw that her life was rooted and grounded in love. Her second husband, Paul, came by sometimes when he wasn't on the road. He was the sort of person people mean when they talk about a character. He was slim and quick and slightly stooped as if he were already leaning into what was ahead. His eyes danced with laughter and mischief. But they were a deep, warm brown—eyes that could be looked into full on. He knew Shirley and loved her. They loved each other in a way I had never seen before, with understanding and unshakable devotion.

After I stopped working for her and moved on to other summer jobs, I lost track of Shirley. But I continued to think of her, slowly realizing as I grew older how I'd let her down at the gift shop. She had needed me to take more initiative and responsibility, to ease her load as she faltered. But I think she knew when we were together that I was blinded by my own troubles, among them the steady dissolution of my mother's life. I was stumbling in a fog of unknowing—unhappy, unconscious of my past, and uncertain of the emerging shape of my future. Shirley was kind and patient with me. Later, as the years passed and I found healing and direction, I assumed that her illness had overtaken her; I never expected to see her again.

The memory comes from a distance, down a dim corridor, or swimmingly, like underwater. The room is large and stark. Sunlight drifts in through tall, heavy-paned windows, subdued.

I am seated with several other university students around a long metal table. The table is bare, as is everything else in this room. At the head of it, a couple in their forties are standing and talking to us. They are our Sunday School teachers, Harvey and Devona Wiederick, at this old, limestone Presbyterian church in downtown Kingston.

I don't remember what they taught us that day, but I can still hear their voices: his deep and measured, hers lively with feeling. I can see her face—handsome, beaming, as she looks at her husband and back at us. "Harvey is so neat," she says. It strikes me, the way she takes such open delight in him. Such delight.

A dimmer, briefer glimpse of her, though a few years have passed. We are in her office at the church. Her face is troubled as she tries to help me. I have come to her because a recent break up with my boyfriend has cracked my heart open and I am tumbling into ruins. The deep pain of my past is starting to be exposed beneath the rubble.

The campus and church groups I have been part of have seemed disconcerted at this kind of distress. There is no solace for me in earnest Bible studies or vast sanctuaries echoing sermons. I bring her my shattered heart, my disillusioned faith, my fierce questions. I sense that she is floundering, too. We part soon afterward, and I don't see her for many years. But something has begun. She has started to pray for me.

I walk along the country road between verdant fields, though the summer in England is waning. All the life around me is robust: wildflowers tumbling along the ditches, ivy covering the walls of farmhouses, thick grass blanketing the pastures. And magic seems to pervade the air in this part of the country just outside of Glastonbury. The mists of morning lie on the fields, and the Tor, that stark ruin atop a treeless hill, is just visible in the distance. I can imagine King Arthur and Queen Guinevere emerging from the mist and cantering past me on this lonely road.

But it is Mrs. Tinney who drives up in her old Volvo and stops beside me. "Do you want a ride to the village?" she asks. "You're welcome to join me."

I have no real reason to go into Street, the next town, but I hop in beside her anyway. She is kindly curious, as she must be with all her guests at Cradlebridge Farm, but especially with a young Canadian woman traveling alone in the quiet reaches of her country. She asks about my parents, and I have to tell her that my father died many years before. I don't know where my mother is. She left my sister and me that summer without saying goodbye or telling us where she was going. After a pause, Mrs. Tinney asks me if I have a boyfriend. I am embarrassed, but I let her know that he and I broke up earlier that year. I have taken the trip to England to help heal my heart.

She is quiet for the rest of our ride, but our shared silence is companionable. That evening, she invites me to go with her to a fashion show at the town hall. I am surrounded by women like her—short, plump, and gray-haired, chatting about the events and concerns of their lives. It is warming to be in their midst. The next morning, the long wooden table in the farmhouse dining room is fully occupied with guests. An American man remarks that we are like one big happy family. As she sets my plate of eggs, bacon, and stewed tomatoes in front of me, Mrs. Tinney says quietly in my ear, "I wish we were."

She is a mother to me when I feel particularly motherless. On my last day in Glastonbury, she drives me to the bus stop in town and helps me unload my belongings from the car. We stand together on the sidewalk, reluctant to part.

"It's rather sad, isn't it, dear?" she says. "Oh, well, you'll come again. And next time, you'll bring your handsome husband with you." She starts to walk away, then stops and turns back to me. "Even if he's plain," she amends, "you can still bring him."

In her circle of buyers and sellers, Lorraine Vos is known as "a picker." Early on Saturday mornings, she scouts garage sales, hoping to buy valuable items at less than bargain prices. She can recognize a certain style of collectible pottery or spy a bit of gold at the bottom of a box of junk. She then sells her precious discoveries, often at an astonishing profit.

When she is not garage-saling, she may be at a park or on a beach with her metal detector, carefully scanning the ground or sand for coins and jewelry. Her explorations usually lead to interesting conversations, especially with children. One recent summer afternoon she was approached in a park by a small boy who asked her what she was doing. "Treasure hunting," she said. He regarded her quietly, then ventured another question: "Are you a pirate?"

When I first met Lorraine, it was at her home in a comfortable suburb of Kingston. That afternoon in April of 1985, she and her husband had their son Ray and me, his new girlfriend, for coffee and a visit. Ray and I had just been to a Good Friday service at a church this family had attended for decades. Lorraine and Walter, both born in Holland, exchanged pleasantries with me in their slightly accented voices as we sat in their living room, sunlight slanting through a picture window onto beige carpeting and soft orange couches. I'm sure we had speculaas cookies or boterkoek with our coffee.

I became especially aware of Lorraine as she asked us for our impressions of the service we had just come from. Her bright-eyed curiosity encouraged candor, so I cautiously described the stifling feeling I had experienced there. She looked delighted. While her husband sat quietly apart in a corner of the room, she probed us further. I confessed how heavy I had felt at the church's emphasis on duty and law. Again, the light of approval shone in her eyes. I didn't realize at that time what I understand now: Lorraine was treasure hunting. And she spied something in me that excited her.

She saw what she would describe as "a hunger for more of God," the kind of hunger that fired and shaped her own life. Soon after this visit, I joined the independent Christian fellowship group that she was part of. She and I became traveling companions on an incredible journey of faith. With Ray, we sought in the sometimes dark places of doubt and the painful places of healing, glints of the jewels of grace and hope.

A cloud of mothers; a cluster of mothers. They came into my life when I was bereft and poised on the brink of my future as an adult in the world. With this benevolent crowd surrounding me, I couldn't wander far into places my brokenness might take me. None of them gave me explicit guidance, but in some mysterious way they held me until and after I met Ray.

He and I embarked together on the long road of faith and healing. After we were married, I spent twelve years at home in our small apartment, not working or studying but remembering and reliving the childhood I had forgotten so completely. The process was very hard, but I had the best of companions. One of them was writer Madeleine L'Engle.

The phone call comes one snowy morning in December, 1994, from an old friend who now lives in New York City. "Come for a visit," she urges. I am afraid and excited. Afraid because I rarely travel and excited at the prospect of seeing my friend and the city. Not least, I know that Madeleine L'Engle lives there. I have been reading her books for years and wanting to write to her, to tell her of the hope and strength she has given me. I agree to make the trip and begin to plan. After writing my letter to Madeleine, I decide I'll try to deliver it to her at the church she is associated with: the Cathedral of St. John the Divine, an Episcopalian church on Amsterdam Avenue.

Later, I am in the Manhattan apartment of my friend, dialing the number of St. John's to find out when the Sunday services are. A man answers. After he provides the information I'm seeking, I venture another question.

"Is Madeleine L'Engle a writer-in-residence there?"

"Yes, she is," he replies.

"Is she currently in town?"

"Just a minute."

I hear a click, then the sound of a woman's voice.

"Cathedral Library."

"Is Madeleine L'Engle a writer-in-residence there?"

"Yes, she is."

"Do you know if she is in town these days?"

"Yes, she is. In fact, you're speaking with her right now."

I am stunned to speechlessness. Then I breathe, "Oh, wow," like any infatuated fan. I struggle to collect myself and speak intelligently. "I'm from Canada and I'm here in town visiting a friend. I've been an admiring reader of your books for a long time, and I've written you a letter." My breath barely sustains this speech.

"What are you doing right now?" she asks.

I grip the table and try to keep my voice steady. "Nothing," I manage. "We don't have any plans for the afternoon."

"Then why don't you come to the cathedral? You'll find me in the library." She gives me directions and we hang up.

We find her in the deepest corner of the old library, at a large oak desk with banks of leaded windows behind and beside it. An elderly golden retriever is resting on the carpet beside the desk. After I identify myself and my friend, Madeleine stands to greet us. I am surprised at how tall she is, at her firm handshake. At seventy-five, she is clear-eyed and forthright, possessed of a radiant strength. She is also crabby. She indicates the piles of letters that line the deep window sills and tells us her family is complaining that she isn't writing enough. Still, she is gracious as she chats with us and accepts my letter. "I will read it tonight," she promises.

Several days later it is Sunday, and again we make our way to St. John's, this time for the 11:00 service. The sanctuary is cavernous and grand. Gray stone pillars thrust skyward to support a vaulted roof; at the end of the building a large circular stained glass window sends glints of blue and red light into the vast space.

The sense of quiet majesty and expectancy grows as the room fills with worshipers and the procession of choristers and priests moves slowly up the central aisle. I glance down at my order of service, and my eyes are caught by the announcement: Sermon—Madeleine L'Engle, author and Cathedral Librarian. I look up in surprise, and there she is in the midst of the procession, walking confidently at her full height. I am struck again by the gift I am receiving.

I am carried in worship, with the rest of the congregation, through hymns, prayers, and readings. Then Madeleine steps up to the lectern and addresses us. As I see her strength, hear her sure voice, and feel the joy emanating from her, I find myself praying for a spiritual realignment. I leave the spiritual lineage of my mother and her mother and hers, women who, in their brokenness, ventured too far into the darkness and became destructive to those around them. I turn to Madeleine and the host of those who have chosen to be servants of Jesus and adopt them as my family. I feel a quiet strengthening in my core. Later in the service, we move into prayers of the people. I pray for my mother, ask God to grant her mercy. It is the first step in a long journey toward forgiveness.

1.6.95

Dear Lori,

What an astounding letter. Thank you for being so willing to share yourself and your life and your struggles with me. One thing you can totally count on: the light cannot be put out by the darkness. We are promised that in the beginning of John's gospel, and our faith is based on that: the light shines in the darkness, and the darkness cannot put out or comprehend it or even threaten it in any deep way, so we have that to sustain us at all times—that Jesus' love and light is always there.

You have come through your horrendous experiences incredibly well, in that your own deep sense of love sustains you and helps you to understand that it is more powerful than any of the evil. That is not always easy to understand; some people reject it. And you haven't and that is wonderful. For every one of us who holds on to the light, there is more light and more hope for the entire universe.

I'm so glad to have had a brief meeting with you and I hope that perhaps, if I'm ever in your part of the world, we'll be able to meet again.

Blessings,
Madeleine L'Engle

We were an unlikely pair: a young Christian woman, not long out of an intense faith community experience, living at home while her husband was working to support her and a woman ten years her senior, a lesbian feminist who would be her therapist. Deb Hudson and I might have missed each other had we let our differences obscure what we shared, a powerful commitment to the pursuit of truth and healing.

We spent twelve years sitting across from each other, looking at and listening to each other. She was still, in a solid, reassuring way. Her rounded body, clothed in loose, colorful fabrics, seemed so settled as she regarded me with her deep brown eyes. Eyes that revealed a patient attentiveness to my words and gestures, to signs of distress that indicated the feeling beneath. She received everything she heard with such calmness that I knew it was safe to be with her and remember.

Well, not remember, technically. I did my remembering at home, in prayer. Late in the afternoons, I would sit at the end of my couch in my small, sunlit living room, cappuccino in hand, and talk to Jesus. I would just talk—head up, eyes open, arm stretched across the back of the couch—not try to repeat some formal phrases I had learned in my church-going days. And occasionally, while I talked about my feelings, struggles and yearnings, and tried to be still and listen, a strange thing would happen. I would feel suddenly wakened to a heightened state of clarity. The shapes of the room would take on sharper edges and I would be alert in a new way. Then I would see a scene from my childhood that I had not even imagined. Some of those memories were truly dreadful, the stuff of nightmares, yet I faithfully recorded all of them and read them to Deb in our weekly sessions.

She heard everything, walked with me through my deepest darkness. And she helped me, with her gentle probing, with the hardest part of the process of healing—experiencing the feelings that went with the memories I was recovering. I remember in one session we were sitting on the carpet together and she was stroking my hair as I cried. I had never been soothed that way before; I had the sensation that a shaft of light was penetrating deep into my psyche with its warmth and comfort. Deb loved me. Although she had days when her eyes were dimmed by her own concerns, her love was constant. It was one of the most powerful tools of healing in my life.

After a few years of work together, she moved her office from a clinic to an open, airy room at the back of her home. I was greeted by her golden-eyed gray cat when I came through the door. Her children grew into teenagers. She again moved her practice, this time to an old downtown limestone building she still rents with other therapists. Our work continued as we confronted and began to dismantle the lies embedded in my memories.

As the darkness of my past slowly lifted and my strength grew, I saw Deb less frequently—twice a month, then once. I became aware that we were spending more time chatting and I was beginning to learn about her life. We were in transition. One day it was time to end. To honor our relationship, I gave her a gift—a photograph of a stone statue of two women bent toward each other. We looked at each other, in soberness and gratitude, for the last time as therapist and client. And, in the rich silence that filled the space between us, we realized that we were friends.

In 2003, my sister and her partner bought a lovely house in the village where she and I had grown up. A particular gift of this place was its neighbors: Shirley, the former gift shop owner, and Paul Sax. So, in a surprising and incredible sweep of fate or grace, Shirley and I were ushered back into each other's lives.

What had happened in our absence from one another? I had married a loving man, undertaken a journey of healing, and found fulfilling work at our city's university. Shirley had survived a succession of serious illnesses: cancer, a heart attack, and the onslaughts and reprieves of the MS she had lived with for so long. Newly reacquainted with her, I found out that she was a painter; she did delicate renderings of flowers on porcelain and large, bright watercolors. She loved flowers. She had a special understanding of the shape of a petal, its softness, the vibrancy of its hue, like she had lived immersed in the shy purple of a violet and could speak its language with her brush.

When I am in the village visiting my sister, I look in on Shirley whenever I can. We sit on her front porch and share coffee and scones—her homemade ones, of course. During my last visit with her, when I went to see her in early September before the university term got fully underway, she led us to the front porch, as always. But she seemed a little shakier than I remembered. Paul hovered a bit longer than usual before he went outside to putter in his vegetable garden. After we seated ourselves, I asked her how she was doing.

"Oh, I'm all right," she said with a weak smile that told me she was not all right. "Hanging in there, anyway."

"What's up? Did anything happen?"

"Well, I took a tumble a couple of months ago and another one last week," she admitted. "The MS is making my legs and feet numb, so I'm not so good on stairs anymore." A rueful smile.

I kept probing, and she let me know that nerve damage to her neck, as a result of the falls, was causing excruciating and constant pain in her face. Often she could hardly eat.

"Oh, Shirley, I'm so sorry," I said, reaching out to grasp her hand. She looked at me and allowed rare tears to come, but only for a moment. She lifted herself a bit higher in her chair.

"Really, everyone's been so kind. The girls have been coming over to help out"—referring to her two granddaughters—"and we think we've found a good chiropractor who can do something for the pain." Then I saw the twinkle return to her eye. "And David hasn't stopped; he played the best joke on us the other day. You won't believe what he did . . . " Her voice grew stronger and full of mirth as she told of her eldest son's latest prank.

Then she turned the conversation to me, eager for my news. But as I talked, I was still marveling at her. I realized again how illness has shaped but not defined her. That twinkle in her eye never disappears for long. It seemed to me that her battles over the years had both strengthened and softened her. Her determination was as fierce as ever but I was increasingly aware of her wisdom, a wisdom that enabled her to deeply befriend herself. She was careful of herself in a way that reminded me of her gentle handling of porcelain pieces in her gift shop. I knew that she gave to so many, besides me, of her time, advice, flowers from her garden, and favorite recipes; at the same time, she treated herself as someone who is loved and worthy of love.

Despite her age (she was now in her late eighties) and her frail health, she was still lovely. Still, hers was the most beautiful garden in the village. People continued to drive on her small street past her house just to see the profusion of life and color: forget-me-nots in the spring, lilies and lavatera, brown-eyed Susans as the summer waned. Still, Paul and her sons, and now her grandchildren, loved her with constant devotion. And still, she and I were blessed witnesses of each other's lives. I paused in my talk, suddenly overcome with tenderness for her, with admiration and gratitude. She just waited for me and smiled.

It is a rare day for early August; the air is clear and light with a hint of autumnal coolness and the sky is intensely blue. Thick grass stretches in a wide swath to the river, which is sparkling in the sun.

Friends and family begin to gather. It is early yet, so only the helpers are here and Devona, my Sunday-school teacher of decades ago, whose house we are using for the day. Nearing seventy now, she is still tall and strong, though her strength has been subdued by nearly a decade without Harvey. She no longer serves as a minister in one of the local churches; she has chosen a quieter life of counseling, traveling, and tending to her family. She tends well those she cares for; her love and wisdom come from a long life of faithfulness to God. Ray and I are glad to be her friends, glad to be here at her home today.

It is a perfect day for a party, Ray's fiftieth. Some of us set up long tables on the deck. Others join the balloon brigade and pin translucent orbs of blue and yellow by their tails to the fenceposts. I see Marianne and Ed enter at the gate, followed by the others from Niagara. Megan is here from Montreal; Mike, Cathy, and young Noah from London. People are now meeting and mingling, and the tables are filling with food—potato salads, condiments, sweet squares. We put great pots of water on the stove in the kitchen for the corn. At the barbecue, Ed gets to work, and the smells of smoke and meat begin to drift on the breeze. Still people come, unfold their lawn chairs, and settle in groups to chat and eat. The sunlight warms their limbs and brightens their faces. It covers them in a glowing mantle as it moves from yellow to gold.

There is Lorraine, Ray's mother, hair whitening, the folds in her round face deepening in a pleasant way after many years of treasure hunting. She sits talking with her middle son's girlfriend. She still snoops at garage sales, searches for gold and coins with her metal detector, and spies goodness often in those she knows and meets. Over the years, she has developed a gift even more wonderful than discerning hidden riches—dispensing generously the treasure that comes to her. She is delighted to give what she has: a quarter to an old woman who needs a shopping cart, a kind word to a student sitting on a bench at the mall, a plot of land to a son who is beginning to find his way.

I turn from the group on the lawn and enter the house. As I head for the kitchen, I stop short at a sight in the dining room. Deb, my former counselor, and Devona are sitting in a pair of winged-back chairs, talking to each other. They are earnest, intent. They are the wisest women I know, and they are meeting for the first time. I stand and watch them for a while. I have been witnessed to life by these women; now I am a witness, simply marveling that they are here. The mothers have gathered again, but now they are my friends. The cloud is dense with blessing.

# PART THREE

# Faith

ROM THE YEARS IN MRS. THOMAS'S CLASSROOM ON, school continued to be a salvation, with the encouragement of teachers and the strength and pleasure that came with my growing abilities. The books I was reading, the lessons I was listening to, the activities I was enjoying, and the friends I was making took me away from home and into a world of some stability and safety, even happiness. Even my father's death by suicide when I was almost thirteen, shock though it was, brought more relief than sadness. And the money he left my mother seemed to energize her. She broke off her relationship with her boyfriend and set about improving our house. She took my sister and me to a decorating store and allowed us to choose the wallpaper for our bedroom, a pattern of ferns that made us feel like we were living in a jungle. One April afternoon I came home from school to find a big pile of manure steaming in the middle of our still-snowy backyard. Mom was preparing to plant a vegetable garden.

Days were filled with school and sports—especially tennis and swimming in the summer—pets and friends, evenings of watching television on the couch, Saturdays of chores and playing at the beach. During the happy times, on a day when sunlight filled our now lovely gold and white living room, my favorite cat was sleeping peacefully on my lap, and friends were coming soon for dinner, I could tell my mother that our home was the best I knew—the most beautiful, the most warm, the most fun.

Another strand of stability was being woven into the background of my life. From early in our years at the new house, my mother sent my sister and me to Sunday School at the little local United Church. There I found a comforting community of benevolent adults, a place where, as the years passed, the stirrings of faith began in me. In the minister's sermons and in the hymns I loved to sing, I heard about good things that appealed to a longing inside of me for purity and beauty. For light.

# You Are All Things Beautiful

You are all things beautiful
naked Joy, blinding Star
enfleshed to meet our weakness
with Your own
Clothed for a time with touch and taste
pain and longing
to call us to a journey
through pain and longing
into naked joy
into all things beautiful.

# The Gift

Stars in all their brilliance dance
their wheeling universal dance of joy
as one extends its shining rays
to light the path of sages through the night.

Angels in bright splendor sing
a strange ethereal music from afar,
calling shepherds from their hills
toward the town where heaven's promise sleeps.

And there amid the earthly din
a baby, new-born, lies in comfort bare
upon his mother's breast. So small, yet
One to bend the knees of human kings
A whisper sent to wake a world
to hope, to love, to know a Maker's heart.

# Communities of Faith

*You quit your house and country, quit your ship, and quit your companions in the tent, saying, 'I am just going outside and may be some time.' The light on the far side of the blizzard lures you. You walk, and one day you enter the spread heart of silence, where lands dissolve and seas become vapor and ices sublime under unknown stars. This is the end of the Via Negativa, the lightless edge where the slopes of knowledge dwindle, and love for its own sake, lacking an object, begins.*

—Annie Dillard, "An Expedition to the Pole"

First, it was a place—a small, plain, red brick United Church, with its sloped roof and modest white steeple—on the main street of our village. Our mother began sending me and my sister there on Sunday mornings soon after the three of us moved to our house by the lake. I suppose, as a single mother, she was eager for time on her own, so the hours we were at church and then visiting with our father gave her almost a full day to herself. My sister and I would hold hands and walk on our own the two blocks to the church's arched wooden doors. Once inside, we were enveloped in the warmth of the sanctuary, with its thickly carpeted central aisle, its golden wood pews, and the softly illuminated cross suspended in front of an ocher-colored curtain in the nave. We made our way to the front pews to sit with other children for the first part of the service, before being let out for Sunday School.

Just before the service, the dozen or so choir members would file in through a side door near the organ, their flowing blue robes making them all beautiful, and take their places facing the congregation. Then there was the call to worship. "Holy, holy, holy, Lord God Almighty," they would lead us, one alto always singing gratingly louder than the rest of the choir, "early in the morning, our song shall rise to thee..." Then the minister would stride in, the folds of his black robe billowing in his wake. Standing in the pulpit, he greeted us in his deep, melodious Irish lilt, full of vigor and kindness at once. I don't remember anything he said during my thirteen years at St. Andrew's, but humbleness and goodness emanated from him, a goodness slightly tinged with sadness. I saw that he tried to communicate the love of God to us in his beautiful voice, but the flow was sometimes restricted by a stutter that made me feel sorry for him.

The church for me was a place apart, its benevolent and stable community so different from my tumultuous life at home. So, second, it was a kind of family, in the way that a watercolor is a painting. The adults, kindly vague and distant, were in the same spots in the same pews every Sunday morning. After some years, I could name most of them, and they knew who I was as they smiled at me and my sister. Together as a congregation we would listen, and pray, and sing. And all the wonderful words of scripture, sermon, and song soaked into my spirit, bringing a comfort that went deeper than my mind could grasp:

This is my Father's world,
And to my listening ears
All nature sings, and round me rings
The music of the spheres.
This is my Father's world:
I rest me in the thought
Of rocks and trees, of skies and seas—
His hand the wonders wrought.[1]

I spent my childhood years amid this pleasant community of ordinary folk. No one ever inquired about my life or sought to know me in any significant way, which, as I see it now, was a mercy. No one came close enough to threaten the split I had created in my psyche to keep my hurt self at bay. The church was a place of comfort, not challenge, and a steady source of comfort was what I most needed. But more, it was a place in which the seeds of faith, like diamonds in the dark, were quietly planted in my spirit. As I learned about Jesus in Sunday School and sang about Him in our children's hymns, I felt stirrings of love in my heart for Him, love that gradually grew stronger as I grew older.

Fair are the meadows,
  Fairer still the woodlands
Robed in the blooming garb of spring;
  Jesus is fairer,
  Jesus is purer,
Who makes the woeful heart to sing!

46

All fairest beauty,
  Heavenly and earthly,
Wondrously, Jesus, is found in Thee.
  None can be nearer,
  Fairer, or dearer,
Than Thou my Saviour art to me.[2]


My love for Jesus became the central fact of my being. It carried me through years of services and Sunday School classes until I presented myself at the front of the church one Sunday morning, when I was thirteen, for confirmation. In my memory, I am standing in a gentle ray of sunlight, my white and yellow gingham dress beautifully illuminated, speaking with pride and fervor the affirmations of my faith. Following that day, I became more involved with my church family, joining a girls' club, attending a Sunday School class for teens with the minister, becoming a member of the choir.

Through the years, the event that was most special to me and my sister was always the Christmas Eve service. One of these occasions, when we were both teenagers, was particularly magical. The darkened church was full of people standing or sitting close together, wrapped in the shadows of evening. Only their faces were visible in the glow of the candles they were holding in their hands and the flickering light from the tall candles in the nave. The poetry of carols and readings caught us all up in the astonishing message of the Incarnation. Then my sister and I stood from among the seated choir members to sing our duet, both of us trying to keep tears from diminishing our delivery of the final verse:

What can I give Him, poor as I am?
If I were a shepherd, I could bring a lamb.
If I were a wise man, I could do my part.
Yet what I can I give Him, give my heart.[3]


St. Andrew's provided me a place apart and a sense of family that allowed me to live, once or twice a week, like a normal person. It gave me respite from the monsters without and the devastation within, nurturing me in the gentlest possible way.

The split I had created within myself, and between my home and away-from-home lives, could not last; nor did it need to. As I grew stronger, the wall began to crumble and the process of integration, though entirely unconscious for me in the early years, began. At seventeen the wall cracked, and I found myself crying uncontrollably in my high school library in the presence of three kind friends. In that empty classroom they then took me into, they spoke to me in a direct way about Jesus that helped usher me into a more conscious relationship with Him. Alone in that room and on my knees, I turned over control of my now unmanageable life to Him. Immediately I felt a powerful sense of being unburdened, and from then on He became the Lodestar of my life, the One whom I follow.

This awakening into a new relationship with Jesus led me to seek the company of others who were as serious about that relationship as I now was. I began to attend the Baptist church of some of my high school friends. The understanding and expression of the faith I encountered there seemed to be more defined, have more substance, than I had previously experienced. People were urged to make a full, surrendered commitment to God. I began to read the Bible regularly and go to Bible study classes. While this church lacked the warmth and comfort of my old United Church, it wasn't comfort that I then needed: it was a more intense, more explicit expression of faith with others who shared my fervor. One Sunday morning when I was in my late teens, I and my sister were baptized by immersion in a tank in front of the congregation. We were lifted, streaming water from our hair and robes, to signify our new commitment to Jesus.

When I left for another city to go to university, I sought out a Baptist church like the one I had just left behind. I found it: a congregation also steeped in Bible study and rigorous teaching. But this community was warmer that the one I had just parted from. The many professionals in the congregation were especially welcoming to us university students. One Sunday I was invited, with several other students, to the home of a doctor and his wife for lunch after the service. I still see the mahogany cabinet she opened for us to choose the china cups we wanted for our tea. This cabinet, set in a dining room of thick white carpeting, was part of a world that was new to me, of quiet, modest wealth, of care in all things, of graciousness, of a deep and steady faith. I felt stabilized and strengthened in that world.

But not altogether genuine. Subconsciously, I knew that the careful conviction surrounding me couldn't speak to the raggedness of my life experience. It was a world of certitude that existed partly by shutting out difference and doubt. During a sermon one Sunday morning, I heard the pastor say that all those in mainline, non-evangelical churches were unsaved, lost. I knew at that moment it was time for me to go. I had spent my whole life trying to be normal, to fit in, yet knowing myself as an outsider. My affinity for those on the fringes made it impossible for me to accept a message that was so narrow and condemning.

I was next drawn to one of those mainline churches—an old limestone Anglican church on the edge of my university's campus. Aesthetically, it fulfilled my need for beauty better than the more modern churches I had attended. St. James was not a large church, but its high arched ceiling created a sense of vastness and openness that was a relief to me. That openness was echoed in the minister's message of gracious inclusivity. The gloom of shadowed corners was lifted by white pillars and pale blue walls, by illuminated, jeweled windows depicting Jesus and his disciples. The space invited worshipers into a kind of reverence that was new to me. In the liturgy of the Anglican prayerbook, repeated week after week, I could gradually immerse myself in the richness and eloquence of centuries-old calls to worship, confessions, prayers, and affirmations. "The Lord be with you. And also with you. Lift up your hearts. We lift them up to the Lord."

In my two years at St. James, I didn't seek relationships. I needed the comfort of solitude away from my busy student life. I went to the Sunday and Wednesday morning services on my own, content to listen to the beautiful words and absorb the mystery and holiness that filled the air like fragrance. And sing. In this tradition, I was able to once again worship in the old hymns I loved. I would look up at the image of Jesus irradiated by sunlight, feel myself surrounded by the congregation but blessedly alone, and sing with my whole self:

Be Thou my vision, O Lord of my heart;
Naught be all else to me, save that Thou art;

*Thou my best thought, by day or by night;*
*Waking or sleeping, Thy presence my light.*

*Heart of my own heart, whatever befall;*
*Still be my vision, O Ruler of all.*[4]

During these undergraduate years at university, my faith life was not entirely solitary, though. Besides attending formal church, I found a campus group that gave me a rich experience of community life. During my first weekend as a frosh in early September, far away from home and overwhelmed, I heard about the Intervarsity Christian Fellowship and decided to go to their outdoor Sunday sunrise service. When I reached the park by the lake, early morning sunlight was touching the crests of the waves, and the breeze blowing in off the water was fresh. A group of students was gathered near the shore, so I began to walk toward them, both shy to meet new people and glad we already had faith in common. One young man saw me and left the group. As he reached me, a wide, open smile lit his face, and he extended his hand.

"Hi, welcome," he said in the warmest voice I'd ever heard. "I'm Roger. We're about to start a little worship service. We'd love to have you join us."

I learned later that Roger was president of the group. His kind welcome ushered me into a community where I knew instantly that I belonged. For the next four years, one evening each week, I would sit on the carpet of a large campus room, surrounded by earnest, hopeful, denim-clad young people like me, all of us coming from various denominational backgrounds to worship and learn together. Here I discovered faith stripped of the clothes of religion, expressed in a relaxed simplicity that comforted me, from the plain walls to the strumming of acoustic guitars to the free-flowing style of the meetings. We listened to stimulating speakers who challenged me intellectually and sang folksy contemporary worship songs that gave me a new way to voice what was within: a growing sense of Jesus as the friend of my heart.

After my second year, I became a student leader of one of our newly formed house groups. Each week, the twenty-five to thirty of us in my group met in a large old rambling house near the heart of campus for a meal and worship time before we split into smaller groups for Bible study. One evening, we had cleaned up after our potluck dinner of stew and rice and gathered again in the main room, some hunkered down on couches, some sitting on rugs on the floor. I stood to address them, elated as I often was to be in this group of like-hearted companions. We were to me like a safe, warm family, and I wanted to embrace them all. Instead, I initiated something new for us, a free-flowing discussion rather than a time of listening to a guest speaker. I sent out a challenging question about what it meant to live by the Spirit and not by religious rules, as the apostle Paul explores in the book of Galatians. After a moment or two of silence, a dark-haired, upper-year philosophy student responded, and then someone replied to him. We were off, grappling with and learning from each other. At the end of the evening, buoyed by our time together, I walked slowly home in the darkness. I was full of gratitude and something more—an intense passion for God. Stopping at one point in the rain-slicked road, I declared to God that I meant business—I wanted to go as far as humanly possible in relationship with Him.

Many of the students in IVCF became my friends, some housemates, and several long-time friends. For three years I lived in a house with five other students from the group. One housemate, a slender, flannel-shirted biology student with long wavy golden hair, expressed a wholesomeness and integrity of person that I admired. Another housemate would send pungent wisps of smoke through the vent we shared and sit cross-legged on the floor of his room, reading poetry to whomever would listen.

In the summer before my fourth year of university, I prayed that God would give me a theme for my final house group that would guide our discussions and study. Soon after, a new understanding came to me of a particular verse of scripture—"You shall love the Lord your God with all your heart and with all your soul and with all your mind and with all your strength . . . You shall love your neighbor as yourself." (Mark 12:30–31 ESV) I caught a glimpse of a love so radiant and profound that I knew it had the power to transform life—my life. I had never experienced that kind of love, but now I knew it existed, and I said yes to it, fully and completely.

Two months later, that love began its transforming work. The young man I had been seeing through my undergraduate years, with whom I had been planning marriage, suddenly broke up with me. He had entered teacher's college and found himself surrounded by new classmates, studying subjects that excited him. He had moved on, and our relationship was a casualty, part of what he was leaving behind. Devastated, I struggled to keep up with my studies and activities, but I was floundering, venturing deep into doubt in a way that concerned the leaders of my Christian group. Several months later, I found out that my former boyfriend was in a relationship with someone else, and I was shattered, any vestiges of hope that we would get back together gone. For two days, my friends took turns staying with me so I wouldn't be alone. Another member of my house group took over as leader.

One evening, though, all my housemates were busy. At odds, I left my house and wandered down my street to the waterfront. I stood watching the waves, gray and buffeted to whitecaps by heavy gusts, crash against the shore. I had never felt so alone and abandoned, so profoundly hurt. It struck me, suddenly, that I was in a dangerous emotional place. So I forced myself to walk back home and immediately called a friend once I got there. She came for me and took me to her parents' place overnight.

I know now that some of my friends didn't understand why the pain I was in was so severe; I didn't understand it myself. Later, I came to realize that the shock of this rejection had opened up my inner brokenness, that inner sense of abandonment and homelessness. And the community life I had been nurtured by had built my strength and faith to the point where I could survive a powerful blow to the wall that kept this past pain at bay.

My faith communities had carried me this far, but no longer was my Anglican church or my campus group enough. I needed a more mature community to care for me in this new wilderness— one that encouraged a more intimate relationship with God than I had seen in the churches and that could handle pain better than a gathering of students. During the summer between my undergraduate and graduate studies, a friend took me to a non-denominational Christian group of about thirty members that met Monday evenings in the classroom of a local public school. The Fellowship, as we called it, was a disparate group of students, middle-aged professionals, blue-collar workers, and elderly folk from backgrounds as diverse as Dutch Christian Reformed and United Pentecostal. What joined us was the desire to be free of the trappings of religion and the longing for an authentic experience of faith. All of us resisted external expectations of our behavior and instead surrendered our lives to the internal healing work of God. The skinny, black-bespectacled pastor, himself a former Pentecostal, taught us about the wilderness journey of the long-ago Israelites in a way that made sense of our struggles. We saw ourselves as a motley band of stragglers being led by God through a process of transformation that would fit us for intimacy with Him. At each meeting I sat rapt, eager for every word of teaching, every song, every prayer, every prophecy. In the midst of my pain I found meaning, and I discovered that the coal of love for Jesus within me was burning more intensely than ever. More, I was surrounded by fellow pilgrims who understood and cared for me.

During one memorable meeting, our worship grew deeply reverent. As a person, we all slipped from our chairs to our knees, and many raised their palms in praise. We sang as those beholding, in the moment, the incredible beauty of God. Later, as we moved into the ministry part of the gathering, I was invited to sit on a chair in the midst of the group. People laid their hands on my head or shoulders and began to pray. One man described a picture he saw in his mind of a glass vase splintered into innumerable tiny pieces. As I sat and sobbed quietly, an older woman prayed for healing and restoration. In the midst of this community, I could stop trying to perform and simply be the broken person I was as God gently but steadily opened my mind and heart to the reality of my past. The people of the Fellowship walked with me as I began the long, slow process of remembering and integrating.

As the group grew with a sudden influx of other university students, leaders in our city's denominational churches worried that we had come under the influence of a cult. They saw our fervor, watched us struggle, and suspected our pastor, who was both charismatic and socially isolated, of building his own small kingdom. In some ways, they were right. The teaching we were hearing about "the dealings of God" left some mired in internal angst for years. Because the pastor seemed to have the most direct connection with God, he became an authority in our lives that robbed some of a sense of agency. I was largely blessed in the Fellowship, though, as this company helped to carry me through the early years of the dismantling of my life and helped to foster my connection with God. And a relationship with a new man, who ended up being my life partner, began and was nurtured there.

Ultimately, though, Ray and I began to see the aspects of the Fellowship's vision that belonged more to fantasy than faith, to recognize that the pastor who had taught us so much about healing couldn't address the brokenness in his own life that was hurting him and his family. So, after we were married, Ray and I left the Fellowship and ventured into the wilderness alone. After the intensity of community life we had just had, we knew we couldn't return to a traditional church. We needed to go deeper into healing and experience with God, and we knew of no church that might support this journey.

At this point in our lives it became clear that the traditional churches we had been acquainted with were not equipped to help those who had experienced significant childhood trauma, though I occasionally tried to look to them for support. One weekend, I attended talks at a local Presbyterian church for survivors of childhood sexual abuse. As I listened to the speaker, I grew increasingly horrified at what I heard. The message was that the healing process started with forgiveness: we had to forgive our perpetrators and ask for forgiveness from God. The church's insistence that the only way to God was through confessing sin and receiving forgiveness, and then forgiving others, slashed through my spirit. I needed grace, understanding, and compassion— not to be forced into asking for a forgiveness I had no knowledge of needing or into granting a forgiveness I was not ready, not nearly ready, to give. During one of the talks, deeply hurt, I simply walked out. And left the church behind.

Accompanied by the few friends and family members who understood and a wise, caring counselor for me, Ray and I were led into the dark places of memory and feeling. For the first several years of our married life, we lived very quietly in our small apartment on the second floor of an old brick house. Ray gradually built his picture-framing business while I cared for our home and healed.

As we traveled this unusual path, we found that we weren't lonely. Our relationship with God deepened as we learned to talk more honestly with Him, felt an increasing sense of His presence, and received the strength we needed to face our fears and pain. This relationship and the support we received from our companions was enough. And continuing our faith journey outside of the traditional church was liberating. One day as I walked the aisles of our local grocery store, I looked around at other shoppers and realized that I was a normal person just like them. The old notion I had learned of the divide between Christians and non-Christians had dissolved for me, and my new perspective of simply muddling along with my fellow humans was comforting. It was a great relief to just follow Jesus as nearly as I knew how and not worry about attending church services or feeling pressured to believe and behave in a certain way. Life became small and safe and protected as we invested our energy primarily in the process of healing.

After several years and with increasing strength, we were ready for the circle of people in our lives to grow wider. I and a former fellow graduate student, now a friend, decided to start a book study group. At our first gathering, six of us, including Ray, met in the tiny living room of our apartment. Four women and two men, all with university backgrounds and ranging in age from our twenties to our early forties, found our places and settled in. Ray claimed his favorite spot on the couch while the wife of the staff worker of the Christian campus group we had been part of folded her slight frame into an easy chair. My friend waited expectantly, her intense blue eyes bright. Then we opened our copies of Madeleine L'Engle's *A Wrinkle in Time* and walked together into a new world. We talked of the way the characters and their fantastical adventures made the invisible, both the noble and the twisted, visible; of the way L'Engle gave us the sense of a more real dimension just shimmering under the surface of life. Our faces and voices grew animated as we discovered a shared eagerness to grapple and learn together, to seek truth.

With this new group of companions, Ray and I explored books, films, and music that led us through the territory of faith and doubt, our fellow seekers sharing our longing for something more.

We also found good companions in the larger community of writers, their characters, and the musicians whose words we studied in songs, novels, poems, films, and books of nonfiction. We discovered others who had undertaken the journey inward, who understood this truth: "How can we see God face to face till we have faces?"[5] It comforted us to hear the call to healing from an author-sage:

We bury for years the tragic memory, the secret fear, the unspoken loneliness, the unspeakable desire...Hard and terrible things happen to us in this world...so we dig the hole in the ground, in ourselves, in our busyness or wherever else we dig it, and hide the terrible things in it...

The good and faithful servants were not life-buriers. They were life-traders. They did not close themselves off in fear, but opened themselves up in risk and hope. The trading of joy comes naturally, because it is of the nature of joy to proclaim and share itself...And so it should properly be with pain as well...We are never more alive to life than when it hurts—never more aware both of our own power-lessness to save ourselves and of at least the possibility of a power beyond ourselves to save us and heal us if we can only open ourselves to it.[6]

The many voices we listened to reassured us that our chosen way was worth traveling, and they stirred our hope.

The years followed, one after another, as Ray and I continued to walk the halls of memory into increasingly difficult places. Still we met with our book group every month, rarely sharing the particulars of our struggles and sometimes even finding ourselves lonely in their midst. But though our fellow members couldn't help us in a direct way, the group served as a container for the words of those who could give us the hope we needed.

A decade passed. A few original members of our group moved away or moved on; others joined and the gathering grew. Still we sought books that illuminated the redeeming work of grace. As the memories I was recovering became darker and even close family members began to doubt the journey Ray and I were on, we found authors whose words guided and sustained us:

The hope on the other side of despair is the unique gift of God to those who walk the journey. It is hope not based on anything in particular working out, not based on pie-eyed religious optimism, not based on mind-over-matter determination. It is a hope that comes to those who wait and walk at the same time. It is not just a hope; it is The Hope; a gift not founded on circumstances or successes but a gift that declares that Reality can be trusted after all...Goodness will win out.[7]

One evening, the group was deep in conversation about a novel all of us loved. We were sitting on fraying couches and wooden chairs in the living room of one of our younger members who lived in the second-story apartment of a large Victorian house. We were grappling with the theme of destiny, taken with the protagonist's fierce certainty about his God-given purpose in life. Her face flushed and her voice raised in imitation of this character, our host read her favorite passage: "YOU'VE GOT TO LEARN TO FOLLOW THINGS THROUGH—IF YOU CARE ABOUT SOMETHING, YOU'VE GOT TO SEE IT ALL THE WAY TO THE END, YOU'VE GOT TO TRY TO FINISH IT."[8] I felt a quickening in my spirit at that call to persevere, a strengthening sense of a possible future full of meaning and purpose.

As the group continued to gather through the years, some relationships gradually solidified like layers of sediment being pressed into rock. Some members left, with or without regret, as their paths diverged from ours. The territory we traveled between the religious and secular worlds was not always a comfortable place for everyone. And once when we studied a memoir of a woman whose past was similar to mine, I exposed some of my pain and loneliness to the group and found I had made a mistake. I had looked to the group for more supportive companionship than it could offer and had to realize that it was not the family I longed for.

Through the decades of our waxing and waning membership, through challenging times and gatherings abundant with life, I have heard voices from the pages speaking courage and urging me on. Their words have shown me the joy set before those who continue on the way toward increasing light and love. The king Aragorn says to the hobbit Sam at the end of *The Lord of the Rings*:

"It is a long way, is it not, from Bree, where you did not like the look of me? A long way for us all but yours has been the darkest road."

And then to Sam's surprise and utter confusion he bowed his knee before them; and taking them by the hand, Frodo upon his right and Sam upon his left, he led them to the throne, and setting them upon it, he turned to the men and captains who stood by and spoke, crying: "Praise them with great praise!"

And all the host laughed and wept... and the clear voice of the minstrel rose like silver and gold, and all men were hushed. And he sang to them . . . until their hearts, wounded with sweet words, overflowed, and their joy was like swords, and they passed in thought out to regions were pain and delight flow together and tears are the very wine of blessedness.[9]

And Madeleine L'Engle continues to point the way: "Whatever we do, we may do thoroughly, with virtue, for we are made by God to be wonderful, wonderful, and most wonderful, and yet again wonderful, and after that out of all whooping!"[10]

These days the group has begun to meet less often as the demands in some members' lives have increased and the priorities of others have shifted. But we are growing in number again. One woman who was with us in the beginning, and always so refreshingly candid, has been able to rejoin us. A new member, a lawyer whose face crinkles with kindness, blesses us with his sensitivity to the marginalized. Their enthusiasm has brought the group new life and energy. And still the characters we meet take us to places we most need to go:

> A circle of grass, smooth as a lawn, met her eyes, with dark trees dancing all around it. And then—oh joy! For he was there: the huge Lion, shining white in the moonlight, with his huge black shadow underneath him.
>
> But for the movement of his tail he might have been a stone lion, but Lucy never thought of that. She never stopped to think whether he was a friendly lion or not. She rushed to him. She felt her heart would burst if she lost a moment. And the next thing she knew was that she was kissing him and putting her arms as far round his neck as she could and burying her face in the beautiful rich silkiness of his mane.
>
> "Aslan, dear Aslan," sobbed Lucy. "At last."
>
> The great beast rolled over on his side so that Lucy fell, half sitting and half lying between his front paws. He bent forward and just touched her nose with his tongue. His warm breath came all round her. She gazed up into the large wise face.
>
> "Welcome, child," he said.[11]

Sometimes a person or community will enter your life when you aren't looking for anyone new and aren't at all aware that you need them. After almost thirty years outside of Christian community, apart from informal worship gatherings at a friend's house we attended every month for several years, Ray and I were certain we would never go back to church. We weren't bitter anymore about the disappointments we had experienced there; we were simply content with our lives as they were and grateful for the close friends we could share our journey with. Still, I was quietly becoming uncomfortable with my own moral smugness in the midst of my circle of left-leaning colleagues and friends, the disdain we sometimes expressed in relation to those on the right. And I still carried deep inside the knowledge that the best things in my life had come to me as complete surprises.

So God picked up Ray and me and plunked us down in a non-denominational Christian community we at first feared might be filled with conservative-thinking fundamentalists. Kingston Christian Fellowship is a country church of about eighty believers housed in a new, expansive brick building with a tall white steeple that also serves as a multi-purpose community center. Sunday services are held in the main hall or gymnasium, where chairs are arranged in a semi-circle and the pulpit is placed on the stage. The people who gather there include retired men and women—a fireman, a nurse, among many others—working professionals and entrepreneurs, laborers, service workers, and several young families.

How God led us there was sneaky. We decided to go to one service for Ray's mom's sake because she had found a place she loved. We went back because Ray's sister had come to town and she wanted to see the senior pastor, an old friend of hers. Then the two pastors, elder and younger, agreed to allow Ray and me to give a presentation to the church on a recent trip we had made to Kenya. For some reason we decided to attend a fourth time; I can only surmise that what was happening there was beginning to creep into our hearts. I found myself, despite my reservations, in the midst of warm, unpretentious people who liked to laugh and clearly loved God. There was no religious formality, just a bunch of casually dressed folk with a longing to know and be known by God, some of whom had been hurt by the church, many of whom were drawn by the startlingly insightful teaching of the pastors. After that fourth service, as I walked slowly through the gravel parking lot, blinking in the fall sunshine, I suddenly knew with certainty that we belonged here.

But that sense of belonging sometimes wore thin. As we kept going back, I felt a strange mix of conflicting emotions. The first was grumpiness. I was really cranky about going back to church and giving up a sacred time of rest with Ray. We had a lovely practice of lying in on a Sunday morning, sleeping late, talking, and just being together in a deeply nurturing way. Once we were both awake, I would nestle into my spot in the hollow of his shoulder, he would draw me close, and we would simply rest together, comforted by the warmth and the regular rise and fall of each other's breathing. I would listen in the quiet to the beating of his heart. Sometimes we would just dose; sometimes we would begin to talk, telling each other about what we were thinking or feeling. Sometimes our talk would deepen into prayer. I didn't want to leave this nest and rise in a rush to immerse myself in community.

I was grumpy also because, though I felt God calling me to this body, I didn't feel that I fit, particularly in terms of social values. The feminist in me balked at the sight of only women in the kitchen and only men in the pulpit. I was appalled at the possibility that women in my new church might actually be discouraged from teaching men, or at least not actively encouraged to develop this gift.

The last reason for my initial crankiness is kind of embarrassing: I felt that being a churchgoer in a community of conservatives wasn't cool. I was used to spending my time with liberal-thinking teachers, writers, and other professionals who had a low regard for Christianity. Spirituality was acceptable, Buddhist meditation was great, but Christianity was the domain of the narrow-minded fundamentalists we all saw parading their hate-filled signs on the news. Lately back in the fold, I was hesitant to tell my friends about the positive aspects of my church experience, about the comfort of being in that community of believers who loved Jesus as I did. I was afraid of their non-acceptance.

Besides grumpiness, I also felt a great desire to laugh when I realized that God had called me back to church, as if God had played some huge practical joke. I had been pranked, and part of me found this hysterically funny. But the third feeling, the one that grew with the passing months, began as a whisper, and I could speak of it only to very few. The feeling was excitement. That God had led

Ray and me to this community was a wondrous thing; I felt like a Narnian would to learn that Aslan was on the move.

But as the months passed and our commitment to this community deepened, I knew I would have to keep being honest with myself and others in order to continue. I would have to confront the senior pastor with my lingering qualms. So Ray and I met with him in his study one dark January evening to hash things out. I was confident that we could all be forthright with each other; this pastor had been genuine and open with us in other talks we'd had, and he seemed enough of a kindred spirit that I felt I could trust him with my struggles. One we were all seated, I drew out a piece of paper on which I'd written everything I needed to say and announced:

"This is my liberal manifesto."

"Okay," he said without a hint of surprise or concern disturbing the kind attention in his round face.

I sat up in my chair and launched into my first point. "I believe that men and women are equally made in the image of God, made to be in full partnership, and equally gifted to preach and teach in the church. I'm deeply bothered that we don't have women teachers here. I think we're all impoverished by hearing from only half of the image of God." He simply nodded, and I continued.

"Ray and I have a number of gay friends who have journeyed with us for a long time. Some of them are married, and I fully support them in that." Again, there was just patient listening and waiting, and I was more relieved by the freedom I felt in speaking my truth.

"I respect scripture, but I don't see it as inerrant or meant in all parts for literal interpretation. To me, the Bible is God-breathed, full of universal truths and a record of God's loving, redemptive intervention in human history. But it was also written by flawed human beings who were shaped by the worldview and culture of their time. So the Bible contains inconsistencies, and laws and perspectives that aren't relevant to our time." A swell of fierce conviction rose from my gut as I prepared to express my final point.

"After thirty years outside the church, I can't accept the preoccupation of the church with who is going to heaven and who is going to hell, with dividing everyone into 'us' and 'them.' How can anyone but God know what is in the heart of each person?" I felt the heat in my face. "I've come to see God at work in the lives of many who don't recognize Him. Jesus said 'I am the Way, the Truth, and the Life,' so as far as I'm concerned, whoever is pursing truth is accompanied by Him." Still the pastor looked unperturbed, so I pressed on, allowing anger into my voice. "I can't accept the us/them judgment that shuts people out and makes God's love conditional. It's dishonoring to God and to the faith journey that so many people are on."

I was done. There was a pause, but a comfortable one, and then the pastor spoke.

"Is that all you've got?" he asked. "We may not agree on everything, but that's okay." Then he went on to share his own understanding of the power and expansiveness of God's grace, and I was the one to be surprised. I had expected to confront a constricting world view, but this pastor's vision of how God loves and restores people opened wider a door to an exciting, hopeful reality.

After almost a year of going to KCF, Ray and I became regular attenders, and I found myself opening more to the life in the fellowship. Our first Easter service was so powerful that it threw me into remembering again the terrible events of a childhood Easter weekend. I found myself longing to tell our two pastors the entirety of my story, including the worst details I usually kept even from those closest to me. My story felt like a stone in my heart that I might finally be able to let go, that might finally be rolled from the tomb of my past, if I told it all at once. The pastors graciously agreed to meet with me and Ray, and we set a date. In the meantime, a visiting preacher spoke at a Sunday service about the resurrection of Lazarus, of Jesus calling forth this friend of his from the tomb. Something was happening.

We four met in the elder pastor's study one golden spring evening. Ray and I sat side-by-side with the pastors across from us, the younger one behind a desk with his ball cap pulled low over his eyes. If he was apprehensive of a tearful telling, he need not have worried. I did relate everything, chronologically and thoroughly— all the significant details of my damaging childhood and subsequent faith journey. But I spoke in a careful, measured way, simply telling the facts without holding anything back. The pastors did not speak. Instead, they listened calmly and attentively, just as I needed them to. At the end, the elder pastor prayed for me. We all stood to leave, and then the younger pastor spoke for the first time. His hat was off, and he looked at me full on.

"Thank you," he said. "It was an honor to hear your story."

"Yes," the elder one affirmed. "Parts of it were definitely ugly, but they were more than balanced by the beauty of your walk with God and the incredible healing He has done in your life." My emotions were strangely muted during this whole experience, but after Ray and I were home again, I couldn't stop singing an old children's song about letting my light shine.

During the following Sunday service, the worship team led us in a stirring song about the resurrection of Lazarus. As I was singing and marveling at the same time, I suddenly felt a hand on my shoulder. A woman I barely knew whispered into my ear, "This song is for you." Since then, I have felt myself walking from my tomb into a community of people who, with their presence and love, are helping to remove my graveclothes, as Jesus commanded those witnessing the emergence of Lazarus to do. In their midst, God is freeing me from all the ways I learned to cope in my life rather than thrive: clenching my body to brace for disaster, blinding myself to reality, pleasing others to prevent further pain, striving for perfection to create order in what I have seen as a chaotic world. As God liberates me from these crippling ways of being, I find myself exposed but held in the company of those who know the redeeming ways of God. "I'm no longer a slave to fear," we often sing together, "I am a child of God." This new sense of identity is changing the foundation of my life.

Now, after three years at KCF, the sense of cultural disconnect is not as strong. On a Sunday, I can leave church, drive back into the city, and walk downtown with Ray without the feeling that I have stepped from a strange world back into the normal one I know. My grumpiness and pride are dissolving and gratitude is taking their place. I am finding myself loving people I would normally have avoided—the retired doctor who seems to resist women in leadership, the recovering addict who sometimes overwhelms me with his need to be known and to be loved. I know that I and my fellow members may disagree about some important issues, but we all desire to honor each other despite our different experiences and perspectives. The church has begun to cultivate the leadership of the women in its midst. In the Bible study group that Ray and I lead, I am learning to fully receive people as they are and to be fully myself in their midst. Together, we are gradually moving into the river of grace that carries us all.

My legs are propped up in the deep windowsill of the old farmhouse at Stillpoint House of Prayer, a retreat center two hours northeast of my town. As I write in the lined green and gold journal in my lap, I glance out at the towering old pine before me and the river curving into the distance. Today, at least half a foot of snow sparkles on the roof outside my window. Deeper snow covers the river in a blanket that ends where the evergreen-clad hills rise.

We have been here since yesterday, my writer friends and I. We come to Stillpoint twice each year for days of quiet and solitude, for writing, and for reading our work to each other. Maureen is a long-time friend from my city who writes and publishes novels, several for young adults. She is the eldest and most seasoned writer in our group, always encouraging of our efforts and keenly astute in her suggestions for making our work better. Susan, newly moved to our town from Toronto, is a short-story and personal essay writer who is finishing a book of memoir. Because of her training as a psychologist and her strength of person, she provides us with a safe emotional space and offers insights into our stories' characters that help us realize them more fully. Rebecca and I are the newer writers in the group, finding our way with writing or just lately venturing into the publishing world. Our youngest member and a career civil servant, Rebecca brings to us her incredible ear for language, her clear sense of what belongs and what doesn't, and her empathy. I hope I bring to these women something they can use from the treasures of my own creative journey.

We met while on a different retreat almost six years ago: the Sage Hill Writing Experience, held in a monastery outside Regina, Saskatchewan. Susan and Maureen were in the novel-writing group while Rebecca and I joined the other beginners learning about poetry and short fiction. An affinity grew between our group and some of the novel writers. Some days, several of us would make the long walk to the small town of Lumsden to buy wine, passing through fields of bright yellow canola or blue flax in the clear prairie air. In the larger company of writers, gathered around dinner tables or talking in clusters outside in the long shadows of evening, I found my tribe. All of us were attempting to write as truthfully as we could the poems or stories we had been given to tell.

At the end of Sage Hill, several of us agreed to stay in touch, and the following year Rebecca found us a new home at Stillpoint. From the beginning, we have felt the peacefulness here, sheltered from the world by the wide river, the surrounding woods and hills, and the quietness inside the farmhouse. We also know that we are held in the prayers of Sister Betty and Sister Pat, the elderly nuns who oversee this place and care for us. And I have found a close faith companion in Sister Pat, who meets with me for an hour each time I am here at the farmhouse. She understands in her bones both the trauma I have experienced and the depth of relationship I have with Jesus. I can tell her every detail of my healing journey, and she listens intently, her clear blue eyes full of light, her response always full of love.

Together through the years, through the sometimes tumultuous and more often joyful changes in our lives, we four writers have become a small community of faith. Though only I would profess a religious faith, with some discomfort at the label, all of us have faith layered into our histories and families in ways that inform our writing and our friendships with each other. As writers, we have faith that we will be able to receive something, from within or without, that we can make into art; we can attune ourselves to the current of the Spirit, or our own spirits. We have faith that we have something to say that might be meaningful for someone else, or meaningful just to ourselves. And we have faith in our little community that we will honor each other's voices as we share our words together.

Last July, in the high heat of summer, we gathered for an evening of reading on the screened veranda at the back of the farmhouse. We hoped for a cool breeze from the river that was shimmering under the setting sun. We filled our wineglasses, which sparkled in the golden light, and settled in. Susan went first, reading in her slow, deliberate way of a woman awakening to the reality of a traumatic accident and her newly broken body. This was Susan's own story, and she had read this section before, but this time we heard more of her thoughts and feelings about the events unfolding around her. Then Rebecca read from her novel, and we were again entertained by the quirks and struggles of a small island community divided by impending development. After the reading, it became clear that the novel, full of colorful characters and lively dialogue, might be better as a series of linked short stories. Next Maureen read from her nearly finished book about a girl hiding and living in her school after escaping her abusive family. We were astonished as we always are by Maureen's skill, at her ability to bring to life a compelling character in such a vividly realized situation.

Then it was my turn. I was nervous tonight because I planned to read about my early childhood, details I had previously kept very private. I had held them back for fear of overwhelming my reader, but it was Sister Pat who had told me: "You can't have the resurrection without the crucifixion"; my story of redemption couldn't be fully understood unless the reader knew what I had been redeemed from. Though I was inwardly shaking, my voice was steady as I sent into the evening air shards of memory that had for so long lived in the darkness. The women around me listened intently, receiving the pain-wracked words, receiving me. Then there was silence except for the low rumbling of thunder; we hadn't noticed the clouds that had crept into the sky. Rebecca was the first to speak. In her clear, quietly authoritative way, she told me how brave I was for speaking my difficult truth. As Maureen and Susan also affirmed the value of my words, I realized that these writer-friends were my audience, the ones for whom I write. In turn, they give me hope that my compulsion or calling to tell my story will be answered by others ready to receive it.

A louder rumbling caused us to look up and past the river to the clouds gathered over the hills on the other side. We all slowly awakened to what we were seeing: a large globe of gray cloud appeared to be resting atop a hill directly across the water from us. But what amazed us was that the cloud was filled with lightning. Every several seconds, it would glow as spikes of white light flashed inside it. Mesmerized, we watched in silence, oblivious to time passing. After a while, we heard the farmhouse door open, and Sisters Pat and Betty joined us to witness the spectacle. As rare and special as this lightning cloud was, it also seemed at home in this place and this company so open to that which gives us breath and takes our breath away.

# Service at Christmas Eve

The signboard lit against the evening darkness reads
"Remember the Christ of Christmas." I wince, leaving
the rural highway and turning in, at this message
to the faithless. But night eases my hesitant way,
cloaks the wide brick building, its pointing steeple.

Church left behind, Babylon has been my good home
for many years, where neighbors are simply neighbors,
not saved or lost, just humans stumbling on a path
of grace or weaving into dark entanglements.
Seeking or dismissing, all together cursed and blessed.

I cross the icy lot to the enclave of the faithful.
Inside, I am clasped in greeting arms. The meeting place—
vast bare hall with rows of chairs—is dim and beautiful.
Branches dangling white stars line the stage; from the ceiling,
strings of bright bulbs, every color, cross over our heads.

The band starts rocking joy; lead singer swings her hips
and platinum hair to hark the herald: her singing, the beat,
the sliding strings above the voices of ye faithful. Still,
a current lifts us all, triumphant, to an ancient awe.
Though nearly stranger here, I am asked to read, offer up
my gift. Then we hear of shepherds met by angels,
these shepherds our guides, too, not cowering
amid their flocks but setting out for Bethlehem.

The service ends; we mingle, murmur Christmas greetings.
Here comes this flock's shepherd, to say he writes, too—
tells of a poem that came to him at a Falwell meeting.
Waits for my nod. But the night is cracked now
and seeping strangeness, this sheep faltering.

Later, sleep-stealing struggle, rising from my bed to seek
my study, dim and beautiful in moonlight. On a chair,
I reach the ceiling's corners, tack up strands of wire,
criss-crossing in the center. I screw in the first bulb,
flame blue: I believe that truth can speak in any voice—
prophet, sage, child, river, hawk. Then yellow, burning:
In some moral matters, I cannot take a stand. Coal red:
Scripture recounts, reveals in myth, poems, history—
Spirit-breathed and mitigated by memory. Green,
another blue: lights are holy fire above my head.

But as I lay in bed again and close my eyes, I see
candlelight instead, touching hair and faces, all the same
as we sing together and linger in the silent night.

# PART FOUR

# Friends

M Y HIGH SCHOOL YEARS EXPANDED MY WORLD AS I took the city bus each day to a school outside my district. There I found friends who were sensitive and creative, like me, and teachers who encouraged me in art, writing, and music. Still, my sister and I rode the rough seas of our mother's outbursts, the times she lost control and hit or shouted at us. Despite having a steady job, a beautiful home, and helpful daughters, she blamed us for a life she still complained was miserable.

The first time I sought help from an adult was one sunny afternoon in the spring of grade nine. I hadn't been able to reach my mother at work all day, and I was worried because of the state she had been in the previous night. I left school early and walked several blocks to the home of my aunt, who listened to my worries. She thought the best thing to do was go to my church minister for help, so she drove me to his house. His wife told us he was away. My aunt then drove me to my home and waited in the car as I went in alone, not knowing what I would find. My body rigid with the dread that was by now so familiar, I climbed the stairs to the second floor. I found my mother in bed in her room, a cross in her hands folded across her chest, an empty whiskey bottle and empty container of pills on the bedside table. She was sleeping, not dead.

Throughout my high school years, between her sudden fits of anguish or rage, my mother seemed to take pleasure in making a good home for us. She particularly enjoyed creating real occasions of special days. On my birthday she would organize a scavenger hunt, giving me and my friends long lists of items to retrieve that would send us all over the city: goofy photos from a photo booth, a nickel from a boy one of us had a crush on. The year I turned seventeen, my party included a Gong Show in our living room based on a popular TV series that featured stellar and sometimes ridiculous amateur talent. One of my friends performed the commercial for the cookie Fig Newtons. Dressed as a huge fig in a stuffed garbage bag, with her long stocking cap and shoes that curled up at the toes, she sang "Ewey gooey rich and chewy inside," she bobbed up and down, "golden cakey tender flakey outside . . . " I heard squeals and gasps from beside me on the couch and turned to see my mother in a fit of laughter, wiping a tear of mirth from her cheek.

To my friends, my mother was warm and funny. In good times, we could invite a couple of friends for dinner; we would all cram ourselves with cabbage rolls and then flake out on the living room rug. Once my sister's best friend, with her vivid red hair and face full of freckles, laughed so hard at dinner that milk shot out of her nose.

But in bad times, the friends my mother usually enjoyed would become a source of resentment. She would rail about the time I spent with them away from home, about all the activities I was involved in, and rage at me for not helping her enough, though through my teens I was cooking dinners, cleaning, doing laundry—trying my best to do all the tasks she required of me. Maybe she sensed she was losing me, losing control over me.

"You're selfish and self-centered," she would snap at me, her words stinging more deeply than her belt ever had, "always having to be the center of attention. Instead of being out with your friends, you should be home, helping your mother." Her voice would rise as her rant reached its climax. "There are givers and there are takers in this world, and you, Lori," she would pause, then end with a rhetorical flourish, "are a taker."

On the emotional seesaw of my mother's moods, I would hear one day, as she spread her arms and smiled, "I love you higher than the sky"; the next, she could be holding a knife to her own throat, declaring, "if this is the only way I can get rid of you, I will." She might have been twisting that knife in my mind. Though I needed her to love me, I never knew, ever, whether she did or not. One thing I was sure of, though: I was not worthy of love.

As our high school years passed, my sister and I continued to cope with our mother's moods alone. Finally, when I was in grade twelve, it all became too much for me. One particular day I was again gnawed by worry because I couldn't contact her at work. During a break between periods at school, after failing to reach her again, I went into the office of a staff member where we produced our school newspaper. As the editor of the paper, I spent a lot of time in this office planning issues, and usually it was a private, comfortable place for me to be. But today two of our younger members, boys in grade nine, started fighting, one hitting the other hard enough to send blood splattering across the table. I didn't know what they were fighting about, and I didn't care. I just had to get out of there.

Overwhelmed and not knowing what to do, I ventured down the hall to the library. There I found three good friends from the choir I belonged to, two girls and one older boy, seated together at a table. I took the empty chair beside the boy and suddenly found myself relating my troubles to them. Then I started to cry as I had never done before. Cry in a way I was powerless to stop. My friends helped me up and led me into an empty classroom across the hall. They closed the door and we sat down and talked quietly for a bit, which helped to calm me. Then one of them, a thoughtful girl with very long, brown hair, brought out a small book from her knapsack. It was a New Testament, and she asked if she could read a couple of passages to me. I was somewhat familiar with the Bible from my church experiences, but somehow what she read seemed new and real and important to me. Then she asked me, so gently, "Do you want to pray?" I nodded. "Would you like us to go or stay with you?" I managed to ask them to leave the room.

After they closed the door behind them, I fell to my knees on the carpeted floor of the classroom and spoke to Jesus for the first time. I told Him my life was out of control, and I couldn't manage it alone anymore. The prayer I prayed was simple and pure: "Jesus, please come in and sit on the throne in my heart. Take control of my life; I put myself in your hands." Somehow I knew in that moment there was someone who understood me better than I understood myself, who knew better than I did what was best for me. In this surrendering, I set a conscious course in the direction of God and all that a life with God meant. After my prayer, I got to my feet and walked out of the classroom, lighter and easier, as if great invisible hands had lifted all the weight off my shoulders. For the first time, I knew peace.

# Friends: Fumbling Together and Full of Grace

How tentative, sometimes, our reach toward each other, how fumbling.
It's a wonder we meet at all in mind and heart. I'll take my cues
from the trees, graceful as they wave together in the wind.
They know the distance they need from each other to thrive,
the pattern their latticed branches should make against the blue sky.

She was my first best friend. I'm not sure what drew us together
in kindergarten, not sure what had formed already in us that laid
the foundation for friendship. I later came to recognize that I have
always been drawn to people who are different, and Margot had
beautiful pink cat eye glasses already at the age of five. I think I
also needed the sense of belonging that comes from commonalities;
she and I were both quiet and thoughtful without being shy. We
also loved art, the vivid swirls of finger paint—always orange for
me, purple for her—or smudges of pastel making beautiful marks
on our papers.

As we grew older, we would read in the small circles of our
flashlights in the pup tent in her backyard or hide behind the couch
at my house, giggling over the statue of David we saw in the *Art and
Man* book we had found. We went to camp in our identical blue tops
with the big white stars on the front, to Sunday school in our same-
style dresses—mine yellow, hers purple.

I don't remember what we talked about; we didn't have the
emotional intimacy of two girls sharing secrets. Because one of my
ways of coping with my troubles was to split off my home life from
my school life, I didn't confide in anyone. For Margot and me, it
was the habit of friendship that we created and were comforted
by. We spent most recesses together, playing hopscotch or double-
Dutch, and went to her house most days after school. She may
have been as vaguely puzzled by my unusual, single-parent family
as I was by her silent, joyless older siblings, her grim father and
valiant mother, all of them living in what seemed much too tiny a
house. But we never acknowledged the undercurrents of strife or
sadness in our lives; we just clung to each other as life rafts on the
surface of troubled waters.

Adolescence was an island that forced us to flow apart. She grew more quickly than I into an awareness of boys and began to hang out with older girls who were cooler than I could ever hope to be. One winter day in grade seven, after almost eight years together, she walked me home and told me she was no longer going to be my friend. I sobbed and pleaded with her, but she was resolute. The death of my father a few months later did not cause me the grief of this loss. Margot and I went our ways and never spoke to each other again.

She was my sister long before she was my friend. Born two and a half years after me, Marianne entered my world just before it shattered into a thousand pieces. Her birth may have broken open our father's anger; I can't know for sure. But while she was an infant in a crib beneath the window in our room, he first came in the night and assaulted me. Our mother found out and turned on me when sunlight filled our room the next morning.

So our sister bond was formed in trauma: I the abused older one, she the tiny witness. I know these small selves from the photos in our family album, one showing my lap full of my curly-haired baby sister as I rocked her in my child-sized chair, and from the stories our mother would tell of her calling for me, "I want my Loli!" I see now that we were essential to each other's survival, but then we weren't old enough to be very conscious of ourselves or each other, not strong enough to build a real connection. Still, her presence gave my life purpose—to take care of her as well as I could.

A few years later, school carried us apart and into friendships with children our own ages. In the summers, from a distance, I would watch her commandeer her two best buddies to help her carry a yellow dinghy several blocks down to the beach. I had at any time one to two close friends and spent much of my time alone reading, riding my bike, or hitting a tennis ball against the side of our school wall. In those years of public school, we shared a bedroom in a home that was sometimes comforting—with evenings spent snuggled under a blue blanket watching *The Waltons* with our mother, or Sundays mini-putting with our father—and always dangerous. But Marianne and I weren't emotionally close; a typical big sister, I considered her of little consequence except during our occasional fights.

Despite the distance, she later followed me everywhere: to a high school outside of our district and into activities such as sports teams and choir. Even into a life of faith—we were baptized together as teenagers during a full immersion ceremony in a Baptist Church. Years later, she left our home city to attend a year of Teacher's College in the university town where I had settled. But even during that year our relationship was stormy.

What turned us from sisters, who were both powerfully connected and strangers to each other, into friends? I think the seeds of friendship grew out of a gift with which we both emerged from our troubled childhood: the gift of a certain innocence that remained intact, a hope in the existence of a world beyond what we knew and of a benevolent Someone at the center of that world. We have always believed that we could, like the Pevensy children, step through the back of a closet into a land of wonder and beauty, like Narnia. Into the presence of Aslan. Our faith has taken us into and out of the church, and still we journey in our own ways toward a life that is more real and illuminated than what we have yet experienced.

Our transition from sisters to sister-friends has required shifts, sometimes painful ones. She has from time to time confronted me about my big-sister ways. One morning, several years after university, the phone rang in my small apartment. It was her; she needed to talk to me about something important. "Lori, I've been wanting to tell you this for a while, and now I just have to say it. I'm finding you very controlling, and it's really hurting me." Her words were an arrow to my heart. After hanging up, I went into my living room and fell to my knees. I confessed my fault and prayed that God would wash from my being the tendency to control others and situations. I knew the tendency was so deep and pervasive that I couldn't master it; I needed God to free me.

Since then and in many ways, I have learned to step back as she has gained strength. Our life paths have taken us in radically different directions—her into full-time public school teaching and mine for many years into a secluded life of inner work. Though we are both still fueled by a desire for wholeness, her path of healing has taken her into an increasingly full and independent life while mine has led me directly into the depths of my own brokenness. I have struggled with our differences, particularly as she has questioned that which I thought we both held sacred, and felt the panic and pain of distance from her.

Still, through all the shifts, and maybe because of them, our relationship has flourished. I have come to appreciate all the ways in which she is stronger than I am and often enjoy the times she bosses me around. A real test of our changing relationship might have been the time when we together wallpapered the ceiling of her bedroom to give it the look of pressed tin. I set about the task in my usual careful way, measuring the ceiling, cutting strips of paper and laying them out to be sure they matched. She eyeballed the situation, relied on guesswork, and plunged in. Instead of fighting for our own way, we found our best tasks and our rhythm with each other and worked in a cheerful, companionable flow until the job was done. Now when we natter about our lives over cappuccino in our favorite cafes, we meet as peers. If I'm discouraged, blinded by the lies or pain of my past to the richness of my present or to a hope for my future, she is firm with me. "That's not logical, Lor," she'll say. "If God has brought you this far, why would God abandon you now?" I have learned that both the closeness and distance we experience with each other, the shared history and the differences of our personalities and unfolding lives, enable us to honor and love each other more.

These days, we continue to cheer each other on, apart in some ways but side by side, as the Aslan of Narnia infuses our lives with what each needs to travel further up and further in. Whenever I have the chance to speak of her, I always say the same thing: "I'm crazy about my sister—she's awesome!" Little brings me greater joy than the sight of her curly blonde hair and green-eyed radiant smile when we are with each other again. My sister, my friend, the delight of my heart.

Peter's presence has graced my life like the sweet, haunting Chopin nocturnes he played when we were teenagers. The precise beginning of our friendship is blurred for me now by the over forty years we have been together. But I do remember singing with several other choir members at his father's funeral when Peter was only thirteen years old. At the time it struck me that, although he was the youngest in his family of five children, he alone spoke, steadily and bravely, to those gathered in the solemnity of the Ukrainian Catholic cathedral to mourn this loss.

The strains of sorrow and beauty wound through and around us, quietly binding us together. Our fathers died when we were young. We took responsibility upon ourselves as serious children of troubled families. Born of immigrant parents, we both struggled to fit in the WASPish middle-class culture of our high school, but we managed to become high achievers nonetheless. And we loved music. We sang tenor and soprano in our school choir, where our director introduced us to pieces by Britten and Willan, to lilting Irish folksongs and grand early choral works. Sometimes after school, I would visit Peter's home and hear how accomplished he was becoming on the piano. Stretched out on a sofa with my eyes closed, I would enter the movements of sound, the contrast in a single scherzo between an aching, tender string of notes and a powerful crash of chords. I resonated with both the sweet sadness and the passion that sounded a deep note in my spirit, an intense longing for freedom and largeness and significance.

After several decades, our friendship is still strong. Much of what has happened in the intervening years we have shared with each other. As a university student, he came out as gay in a quiet, tearful, holy conversation between us on a park bench in the gentleness of darkness. He let go his dream of becoming a concert pianist and turned to law. I married and he did, too, some years later; then he and his partner divorced soon after. I gradually became a teacher and then a writer. We continue to visit each other several times each year and have long phone conversations in between. Peter has become like a brother to me, comfortingly, steadyingly familiar; together we speak in the kind of shorthand used by those who know each other's histories well. We cook for each other, open bottles of good wine, share details of the lives of those we love, watch each other age as our hair becomes whiter and bodies more rounded.

Sometimes when I visit him in Toronto, he plays a private recital for me. I arrive at the door of his condo and he ushers me into his living room where the table is laid with cheese and wine. We talk lightly of recent news in our lives. Then he takes his tall frame to the grand piano at the end of the room and I swing my legs up onto the couch. He flexes his fingers above the keys, lowers them, and begins to send notes swirling into the room. I close my eyes and am lifted on a wave of sound, a wave that swells and falls and carries me into prayer. Sometimes I open my eyes to see his hands flying over the keyboard, too fast for thought. Today he introduces me to pieces I haven't heard by Mozart, Schubert, and Liszt. I especially love the waterfall passages of Liszt.

The music fades and we sit in silence for a moment. Then he returns to the table and I reach for the pages I have brought, settle them in my lap. I have not been writing as long as he has been playing piano, so my voice is more tentative. Still I try to speak from the river that lives inside of me and words fill the room: a poem about Lazarus emerging from the tomb, a story about an old man and the legacy of his orchard. At one point, I look up to discover that Peter's eyes are closed; he is soaking in words as I have been steeped in song.

To finish this time of offering each other our best gifts, Peter has a surprise for me. He walks back to the piano, seats himself, and smiles at me before his fingers lower once again. The familiar notes of the favorite nocturne he played when we were young drift into the room. My breath catches; tears spring to my eyes. Again the strains of sorrow and beauty bind us close but deeper now because we know these notes so well.

Often in our thirty-year friendship Ruth and I would laugh and say our relationship could never end because our whole lives would fall apart. Together we had formed and were guiding several communities: a book study group, a writers' group, a small worship gathering, and the classes of students we coinstructed. We could laugh at the idea of our friendship ending because of our certainty that it never would. Deeper than our shared involvements was the faith that ran so deep in both of us, the foundation of our friendship. Our activities formed the walls of a house we were convinced could not be shaken.

That we became friends at all surprised me at first. As graduate students, we found ourselves in the same cold, dark basement office of our university's humanities building. Unlike me, Ruth was quiet and studious, always prepared for class. She sat bent over her books in a little carrel, steadily making her way through the mountains of material we had to read each week. With my books and papers covering a wide table along an adjoining wall, I was struggling to keep up, and her industriousness and natural reserve intimidated me.

But Ruth and I found ourselves two of the very few people who stayed in our town after completing our degrees, a circumstance that moved us closer together. Soon, we had started a book study group of like-minded women and men interested in good stories, challenging issues, and experiences of the faith journey. We were seekers who gathered to grapple with and be edified by books of fiction and non-fiction, films, and music, all of which we hoped would confront the dark realities of life while holding out hope for redemption.

As we explored themes of the faith journey together in our book group, Ruth and I began to meet regularly to share our lives. As women so often do, we talked earnestly over coffee and scones at one of our local cafes, becoming so immersed in each other's lives that the bustle around us seemed to cease. I came to understand that the reserved, quiet woman from small-town P.E.I. had deeply felt sensitivities and a fierce loyalty to both God and the people at the center of her life.

We both married. She continued her work at the university's writing center as she had one child and then another. My life took an unusual turn as I withdrew from the world into my home and a long period of inner healing. I don't and will likely never know what she thought of the path I took then. But whatever questions or qualms she may have had, she kept them to herself and simply walked with me through those dark years. I shared with her the worst details of the memories I was recovering; she listened with her intense blue gaze and the quiet steadiness of her presence. It never occurred to me to wonder what hearing those memories might have cost her.

After some years, when I began to work at the university in the same capacities as she did, our friendship became layered with coteaching and later with the cofounding of a writers' group and a small worship community that gathered in her home. Still we met at cafes to confide in each other our challenges: her learning to care for her children as their special needs became apparent and I balancing ongoing memory work with new responsibilities in the world.

Several years ago, our friendship suddenly developed cracks that widened astonishingly quickly. Ruth began to question my behavior in two of the communities we were part of. Whether or not that behavior was appropriate and whether or not it needed to be addressed, the scrutiny and challenge were too much for my still shaky sense of self. The more we attempted to resolve our differences, the deeper the cracks became until our relationship tumbled into ruins. What we had joked about for years had come to pass, and we began to dismantle the shared commitments that weren't necessary to our lives and livelihood. The process, as with many separations, was deeply painful.

Since then we have continued in a relatively easy way to deliver the course we coinstruct and in a less easy way to attend our book study group together. As colleagues, we can communicate exclusively through email; in a book study gathering we meet face-to-face. We are slowly becoming comfortable in each other's presence again. I have come to a tentative new perspective only distance could have afforded: perhaps our friendship simply became too hard for us. As the healing work has continued in my life, I have come to see that a very old coping strategy of mine has crippled many of my friendships, the relationship with Ruth possibly most of all. Like many traumatized children, I bonded powerfully with the parent who was most capable of caring for me: my mother. I so fused with her that I completely lost my sense of self. That tendency to bond translated to friendships in which I pushed intimacy when it was not appropriate to try to make myself safe in the world. Although I don't know her perspective, it's possible that, in sharing my full history with Ruth, I put too much weight on her; with the addition of some challenges in our communities, cracks in our relationship might have been inevitable.

Very recently we met, both tentative, to discuss the repercussions of our split on our book study group. I was not expecting to talk about what had happened to our friendship. But we found ourselves among the ruins, again resisting and bruising each other, when suddenly a path opened in the rubble. I began confessing my new knowledge of that old pattern, and she let me know how I had leaned on her too heavily at different points in our friendship when there were difficulties in our communities. I heard the truth in her words and told her how deeply sorry I was. Once again her blue gaze met mine as she received my regret. We could see each other again. This gift of clarity returned us to the foundation of our friendship, a foundation that was always deeper than our shared involvements, our best intentions, and our most damaging blind spots. It rests in the One who knew us both before the foundations of the world and who will open a new way of relationship before us.

When I envision us together, this picture comes to mind: We are sitting side by side at the end of a dock, our feet dangling in the water. Soft and gentle, the air holds no wind. Late afternoon sunlight lays a golden path on the quiet surface of the lake. All is still; the only movement is the easy rise and fall of our breathing and the ripples our feet make as they stir the water. Our forearms touch lightly and my head rests against His shoulder. We do not speak. Our understanding of each other and who we are together fills our shared space; the silence that enfolds us is all we need for words.

A surprising gift: my sister's friends became my own. First it was Cindy, the shy, sweet girl who was my sister's best friend from the time they were in grade three. Cindy and I began connecting at the end of our university years when she lost her mother and found herself alone, her father having died much earlier. In those tumultuous years, we drew together for the comfort and belonging both of us craved. When I went back to my home town to visit my sister, I began to have dinners out just with Cindy, and through the next two decades those dinners felt increasingly like communion. The wine and food we shared while looking at the sun set over Lake Ontario symbolized our experience together of drinking deep a mysterious cup of grace and being fed with sustenance for our spirits. As we told each other our struggles— hers with long singlehood and later health issues—I discovered her strength. She was steadfastly loving in our friendship and able to hear with full presence the memories of childhood I was recovering. The surprise to me was that my little sister's shy and quiet friend, so often in my sister's shadow, became one of the few people in my life whose strength allowed me to be entirely open and vulnerable. Meeting with her felt like stealing away to a holy place of deep intimacy. Cindy died just short of her fiftieth birthday, and I hope I provided as good a home for her as she gave to me.

Chris, the third member of the trio that included my sister and Cindy, also became my friend. I often stay with Chris now when I visit my home town: her house, unlike my sister's, is cat-free, and it is also ordered and serene, a quiet haven. Late in the evenings, often after a dinner out, Chris and I like to snuggle up under blankets on the couch and loveseat and have a cup of tea together. As Cindy surprised me with the strength of her caring presence, Chris astonishes me with the quickness and depth of her understanding. She is able to listen to aspects of my past and my healing journey with a loving interest and calmness, while I hope I offer her insight as she grapples with the conundrums of work and relationships. We are patient with each other and interested in every detail of each other's lives. As with Cindy, we see each other only a few times a year, so we seem to meet in a place apart from day-to-day realities, a place we create for each other to connect with ourselves more deeply, be loved in our vulnerabilities, and find new perspectives.

I know now that my need for intimacy, for home, can be misplaced or burdensome to others, so I tread more lightly now. That need has also lessened as I have healed and befriended myself more deeply. The extraordinary sharing I have experienced with my sister's friends who became my friends is a fragile and precious gift I receive with gratitude and the hush of wonder.

It seemed that she dropped straight from heaven into a wooden chair across the table from me at a roadhouse restaurant near her father's country church. Ray and I were visiting friends who took us to a service at this little church and to meet the minister's family for lunch afterward. Megan was the eldest of the two daughters and a student at the university I had attended over a decade earlier. She was here visiting her family for Thanksgiving.

Our first conversation sparkled with an immediate affinity based on shared university experiences, a love of books, and a bent toward deep, honest talk. But that affinity went beyond our common interests: somehow we recognized each other with a clarity and delight that seemed to bubble between us from another world.

Two weeks later, back in our university town, Megan came to my book study group for the first time, and the following month she led us in a study of Shusako Endo's novel *Silence*. Her fearless questions took us into intense grappling about matters of faith. Shortly thereafter, I decided to ask her out for coffee. I don't remember what we talked about, but I do remember being so overwhelmed with excitement that I had to run all the way home.

I might have been intimidated by Megan's sparkling brilliance except for another aspect of her character that I soon discovered:

her tendency to do really goofy things. Sometimes, her exuberance and heavy reliance on intuition lead her away from caution and into funny situations, like running for a bus with her tights sagging to her knees and making a quick diversion to the nearest bush. A few years after we met, she set out driving from our university town during a Christmas break to visit her family in southern Ontario. She drove for more than an hour, intent on keeping to the road as snow swirled around her little car. Then a sign loomed up beside the highway: Montreal 100. She had driven east instead of west.

"It was terrible, and then it was okay," she told me afterward. "I drove back to Kingston, hopped on a train, and met a really cute guy in red velvet pants. We talked all the way to Toronto." I won't forget her delight at the usefulness of the map of the Underground in London. "It's amazing," she said with the breathlessness of discovery. "Maps actually show you what's coming next!"

After her undergraduate degree, Megan moved from our city to Montreal to take a teaching position. Our new geographical distance was hard for me, but we visited each other often in those early years and our closeness continued to grow. When she had lived away for nearly five years, I decided to spend a weekend with her in the transitional apartment she shared with two women she didn't know well. Grateful that they were both away for the weekend, we settled on the futon in her long, dim, pine-floored living room for tea and a chat. We covered our usual topics: the physical details of our lives, our teaching work, our faith, our relationships. She told me of her struggles to find community, a gang of friends with whom she could belong and on whom she could depend to be there for her. She still felt isolated and lonely in this big city.

Our talk continued to deepen as I related details of the healing work that God was doing in my life. But as I spoke something else was pushing its way to the surface. Ray and I had been trying for a year and a half to conceive a child despite the fact that I was now in my early forties. We knew our chances of conceiving were slim, but we wanted to receive this gift if God had it for us. Now, though, in talking with Megan, the knowledge that the time of trying was over suddenly came toward me like a train rumbling into view. That train hurtled at me until it hit me full force. I would never be a mother. I felt myself break open: a wail rose up and split the room. Then Megan reached for me and pulled me to her as the torrent of grief came. She said nothing but stroked my hair as I sobbed in her lap. In the quiet of that place, in the care of this friend who loved me and could handle my pain, I was safe enough for the terrible truth to come to me. She held my grief as only my husband and my counselor had ever done, as I have done for her since then.

As the years passed, I watched Megan complete two graduate degrees in education and ultimately become a teacher of teachers. With her insight and energy, she could spur both students and teachers to reach beyond their limits. But with her life changes and the new physical distance between us, our friendship began to diminish. From the luxuriousness of time and the easy intimacy we shared during her last golden summer in our town, with regular Chardonnay-enhanced dinners in my back yard, and the frequent visits of her early years in Montreal, we moved to snatching occasional phone calls and rare short trips to see each other. I struggled harder than she did to adjust, fighting feelings of rejection and insecurity, while she felt the pressure to try to keep up her end of the relationship.

Finally, after years of me feeling forgotten or lost in the whirlwind of her life, she came for a visit and we had it out. We settled across from each other at an outdoor table of my local cafe. The clouds hung dark and heavy with rain; the air was close. I began by expressing the hurt I felt as she careened through life and left me in the dust. We had walked together through similar emotional and spiritual journeys, enjoying a rare and wonderful understanding, but now our friendship seemed stretched too thin to sustain such closeness, such deep sharing of our hearts. This was my familiar refrain, and I quickly saw that she was not accepting it this time. Her voice when she responded was full and clear with an undergirding of anger.

"I hear you," she said, "and I understand how you feel. But I can't meet your expectations. I love you, and I want our friendship to continue; as far as I'm concerned, I'm in this for life. I hope you can accept that and accept what I have to give. My love for you and the time I have for this friendship is what's on offer: take it or leave it."

The bracing slap of truth hit me full in the heart. It knocked something into place, and I was finally able to accept the solidness of who we were to each other. Since then, her life has continued to expand—with a husband, child, and new career—as mine has built more slowly and quietly. But my belief in our love for each other no longer wavers. And along with the new steadiness is still the joy of being together that sparkles like sunlight dancing in the waves.

She is a writer who, over the past decade of our friendship, has ushered me into a life of writing. Occasionally, when she tells me of a new writing opportunity she thinks I should pursue, her words ring like the call of a prophet—a call I can't ignore to become more than I understand myself to be. She is also like a rare bird, one who loves its freedom, so I have learned not to expect an easy or consistent intimacy. As she is always just who she is, I am learning to be just who I am—more truthful. We love each other in part because we love truth deep in our bones and help each other trust the truth we know. When she is able to be fully present with me, we share a depth of feeling and clarity of insight that is also rare in my life. And we share joy, a joy in being and being together that I sometimes see as a smile lighting her handsome face, a flash of radiance.

Without knowing it, Maureen has been teaching me about love and distance, showing me that significant, transforming love does not have to be expressed in the kind of emotional intimacy I have always sought.

Often a small vase of flowers sits waiting for me when I arrive at the writing studio early on a Friday afternoon. The tiny bouquet is a lovely, punctuated reminder of her presence, but really while I am here, I am surrounded by her. Physically, she is writing or puttering in the house I see through the screened door of this converted tool shed that is the studio. The house, a long, low cottage with a red tin roof, was where she grew up and where she now lives alone. The mature oaks and pines towering over the house and shed are her trees; the view of the river I see out of the window is her view.

She has given me this place to come to every week to write to the sound of the wind in the trees and the rhythmic shushing of the river. It is a place of stillness and peace, a sanctuary. The old tool shed is actually a sturdy little building with solid walls and a red brick fireplace. She has painted it and filled it with a futon, shelves, two desks and chairs, art and mirrors, so it is a pleasant and comfortable space in which to connect with myself and create.

Her invitation to begin coming to the studio a couple of years ago marked a new stage in our friendship. When we met eighteen years ago, she worked at the university Writing Center that I was joining as a tutor. Several years later, as managing director of the center, she evaluated my performance. Her feedback was brief: "All you need to think about now is how to make this work interesting enough for you to want to stay." Her kind words when my mother died that year also surprised me: "I hope she realized what a blessing her daughter was." Maureen woke me to a new understanding of myself that was far more positive than I was capable of coming to on my own in those days and years. And I came to learn that she mentored many, many others besides me.

Maureen is the most gracious, elegant person I have ever known. Tall and straight, she wears flowing tunics of cotton and linen in her easy, natural way. Tortoiseshell glasses lend a scholarly look to her lovely face softly framed by her bobbed white hair. Her elegance and graciousness are not the brittle kind that come from privilege; they don't carry even a hint of condescension. I think she is more at home installing shelves or pulling out garlic mustard weeds in her woods than engaging in witty banter in a crowd of influential people. But she carries herself well anywhere and with anyone. Her graciousness to all she meets, particularly to the young, particularly to those of us who have been especially broken, seems to come from a deep well of understanding and empathy. She quickly defends what most of us would see as incomprehensible behavior, except when a line has been crossed for her and she bursts forth with her rare, indignant "Well, excuse me" that causes those of us who love her to chuckle.

In her mentoring of me, I have been changed by the quiet undergirding of her positive regard. Her gift of the writing studio shook loose what remained of my concept of myself as one not worth giving good gifts to. That first afternoon, after receiving the key from her, I let myself in and simply sat there on the futon for what seemed like hours, looking out the screen door at the trees waving in the wind, then out the window at the sparkling river. I wanted to receive as deeply as I could the beauty and kindness that had come to me.

The little tool shed is as sacred a place now as it was that afternoon two years ago. These days, my writing time is embedded in a routine Maureen and I enjoy every week. I park my car and knock at the door of her house. She calls out to me; then I go in and greet her, offering up the small treats we'll share after our writing time. Then I spend a few hours in the studio, coming to the house once for a washroom break, while she writes in her dining room. At 4:00 we meet up in her kitchen for lattes and spend a very pleasant hour chatting about big things and small, like sisters do. I am careful not to share the more painful aspects of the healing work that continues in my life; I sense that she could be uncomfortable with this and I don't want to overwhelm her. After our chat, I leave for home. Each week, I am struck by a funny peculiarity. When I look at myself in her bathroom mirror, I always appear more beautiful than I know myself to be. At first I thought it was a trick of light or the angle of the mirror. Now I know it's her.

# PART FIVE

# Family

T HE YEARS FOLLOWING MY CONSCIOUS ENTERING INTO relationship with God frothed with growth and change, change that took me steadily away from home. During twelfth grade, when I was seventeen, two of my uncles took me aside during a family barbecue on the farm to give me advice about my future. They urged me to accept my grandmother's offer to send me to a private school for grade thirteen so I would be as prepared as possible for university. Though I loved my friends and teachers at my small suburban high school, I heeded my uncles and went as a day student to a prestigious private school in my hometown the following year.

When I drove through the iron and stone gate that first day, I entered a world that was starkly foreign to me: of old brick residential and classroom buildings enclosing a large grassy square, of archways and ivy, of wide groomed playing fields, of a line of expensive cars gleaming in the sun. The students I encountered also seemed impossibly manicured, with their polished appearances and gloss of confidence. I couldn't imagine them understanding a life with an unstable single mother who sometimes had to scrounge for grocery money. All I could do was hope to avoid standing out as I daily made my way to my classes. I was challenged in my studies in a way I hadn't faced before, in an old boys' culture of privilege that was intensely alienating to me. My only place of refuge was the chapel. If I had time between classes, I would steal down a stone passageway, heave open the creaking oak door, and slip inside. Then I would sit in a pew warmed by sunlight filtering through tall stained glass windows and soak in a silence infused with the presence of God. Often, I would stand in the aisle and begin to sing, knowing that there was no one around to hear me, the most beautiful hymns and songs I knew. I loved the way my voice lifted to the high rafters and reached, I hoped, to God's heart.

Besides my times in the chapel, the best part of this year at private school was that it carried me into a future that was right for me. The school allowed senior students a week away to investigate university campuses, so I set off in the little car my grandmother had given me with three boys from Hong Kong to tour colleges all over Ontario. I had come to know these boys because we played on the school's badminton team together. My companions wanted to visit a university in Kingston, the furthest city on our tour from my hometown, so we ended there. When we reached the city, we separated—the boys meeting some friends and investigating the engineering department and I exploring on my own. As I stood alone on campus that evening surrounded by old limestone buildings, large, soft flakes of snow drifting down around me, I was visited with a quiet conviction that this was the place for me.

So the following year I left my mother, my sister, and my home behind, traveled four hours north-east, and again entered a new world. University life teemed with movement and stimulation. I learned to navigate through the campus, entered disciplinary studies that were new and exciting to me, and adjusted to life in residence. Though I again encountered privilege—my roommate was from a wealthy Toronto family—I also found others like me, able to attend university only because of grants and loans and summers of hard work. Though this new life was often strange and overwhelming, it was also liberating: I was free to make my way in the world without the daily weight and stress of my family.

For the first four summers between school years, I continued to return home to work on my uncle's fruit farm and take other jobs, one a very good office job with significant responsibility. But during my final summer at home, between my fourth year and graduate school, it became clear that my mother's life was dissolving. She had been let go from the bookkeeping job that had grounded her for nine years and then lost a subsequent bookkeeping position at a failing bakery. Now she was working as a live-in cook for a wealthy woman in an historic neighborhood not far from our apartment building. She had also started drinking heavily again. One night my sister and I received a phone call from our mother's employer who had taken her to her vacation home on Lake Erie. Our mother had become drunk and unmanageable, and we were to retrieve her the following day. I drove out to get her alone, my body tight with the dread I had known too many times before. During the ride home, I spoke to my mother as I had never dared to do, telling her that she would risk losing her daughters completely if she didn't agree to family counseling. Our first and only session failed spectacularly with her sweeping indignantly out of the room.

Jobless, she now spent time with her new, equally struggling friends on a downtown street corner, sometimes wandering drunk into the office where I worked. She was adrift, desperate. And I could no longer help her. One afternoon after she stumbled out my office door, I stood in the window watching her go and felt something break inside of me. I was done. For my own sake, I had to give up trying to take care of her. If she chose to take her own life, quickly or in a more gradual descent into self-destruction, that was her decision. She was not and couldn't be my responsibility anymore. I was my responsibility, so I stepped into taking my own side and let her go.

Soon after, I received a call during the day from the manager of a local hotel, urging me to come and get my mother, who was creating a disturbance. I left work and drove to the hotel. I found her in the lobby, talking loudly and hanging onto the arm of a man she said she had met in the government unemployment line. They were about to leave town together. I begged her to stay, but she shouted at me to go away, to stay out of her life. I turned without a word and walked out of the hotel.

My sister and I didn't hear from her for several months, and we didn't know where she was. Despite the strangeness of abruptly finding ourselves all on our own, we also felt a great sense of relief. And after that summer, I began to live year-round in Kingston. I wasn't able to be conscious of abandoning my sister, but that abandonment had begun years before. At this point in my life, the process of becoming free of my past, at least circumstantially, was fully underway.

# Hands

I look down and see my mother's hands—
the same long fingers, square-tipped,
the bony knuckles, blue ridges of veins
rising beneath the skin. I cringe a bit
when I see my thumbs tucked in like hers
hands trying to make themselves smaller,
less exposed. I don't want to clutch them
to my body as she did, hands hiding,
excusing themselves.

I look down and see my mother's hands
but not their size; mine are smaller.
And not her club thumbs, and not
the chafing redness from so much scrubbing
and digging, so much grasping, so much
never enough. She used to plunge her hands
into harsh or hot liquids, nick them often,
as if they didn't quite belong to her,
could be abused, like me.

I look down and see my mother's hands,
but I want to see my own. Not hold them close
but move them out, give them their space,
their place. Extend them, open-palmed,
to the sky. Hands of mine, be brave, stay open,
stay open.

# Wellspring

One of my favorite places on my grandmother's farm was the well behind the farmhouse. I say it was my grandmother's farm because my grandfather's presence seemed so peripheral in my experience there. She was the one. showing my sister and me how to grasp the end of a cherry tree branch with one hand and twist the green stems with the other, who commanded, "You pick all off!" She was present in the barn, packing peaches in the heavy Niagara heat, or at the stove in the kitchen, the ironing board in the hall. In the daily life of the farm, my grandfather was a silent figure sitting at the kitchen window, looking out over the orchards. Inscrutable, stern, his face allowed no interruption, no violation of a solitude so quiet and impenetrable that he might have been back in his native Estonia before the war surveying his fields.

But the well. It was in the middle of a lawn that ended with the barn on the left and a line of rosebushes on the right, with an orchard of peaches stretching out beyond. I liked the simplicity of this small structure: the pump's metal rods rising from a hole in the circular cover of whitewashed boards, the cement wall beneath. Nearby was a dented tin cup for dipping and priming the pump. I loved the feel of the pump's smooth wooden handle, the rhythmic downpull and uplift as my arms strained and released. When the water came, it was a strong, clear flow from the spout to the bucket hanging beneath. I can still hear it pattering and pounding the bottom, see the bucket swinging until it became full and still.

I don't remember distinctly what we did with the water we drew. The farmhouse had indoor plumbing, so we didn't have to cart pails full inside. I know my grandmother soaked the soil of the red geraniums in her garden. And there were moments of our concentrated gulping from the tin cup on hot, dusty days of picking. On those days, the water was startlingly cold and pure, with a taste that hinted at the metal bucket and the minerals of underground.

Near the well was an old apple tree, with its short trunk and wide canopy of thick branches. It was easy to clamp my hands on the lower limbs and hoist myself up. I leaned against the tree's arms that were sloped as if made to hold me. The branches were as solid as the wellwater was pure and clean. They were among the simple constants that made the stern silences and harsh words, the vagaries of human failing, less likely to reach the groundwater of my soul.

The idea of a well later became important to me when, in my early twenties, I started attending an independent Christian fellowship group. There I was introduced to the idea that God could transform my life. Heal it to the very bottom. The group was an odd assortment of about fifty people—working people, retired folk, housewives, university students, a couple of professionals—mostly people who in some way didn't fit the mainstream and who wanted more than they could receive in conventional church environments. We were dreamers, I guess. We must have looked like a pretty rag-tag group in many ways, but I didn't care. What I heard there—about journeying through a spiritual wilderness and being changed in the process—enthralled me like nothing ever had. I needed healing. I wanted to be transformed, made new. I wanted to know and be known by God as fully as humanly possible.

We often used a metaphor of a well to help us understand the process of healing. The idea was that each of us had within a spring of living water that could fill the well and renew us and others. The trouble was that rocks and debris had clogged the well and contaminated the water. The debris of our lives consisted of the scars of abuse, broken relationships, disappointments, bad decisions, and the resulting kinks in our character that diminished us. What we needed to surrender to—and many of us did with our whole hearts—was the activity of God opening the well to the light, removing the rocks, cleaning out the sludge, and restoring the water's flow.

As a child of chaos, I have always yearned for permanence. Even now, I have trouble with the changing of the seasons. My feelings tug me in two directions each March when daylight is stretched and tiny sprouts of green appear in my front flower bed. I am elated by the new growth pushing through the rotted leaves of last year, and I eagerly clear its path. But it saddens me to lose the long evenings spent snuggling with my husband and watching television on the couch. Warm under the Hudson's Bay blanket and nestled beside him, I peer across the snowy street to see the flicker of the neighbor's screen through his front window. Winter gives us a reason to rest, to sink into the comfort of our homes and each other. Spring means industry and movement and I am never altogether ready for it.

Spring also means the end of the school year. At the university where I teach, the last day of classes is usually early to mid-April. I have trouble taking leave of my students. I spend eight months learning to understand them, learning how they need to learn, occasionally hearing or reading about what moves them or what they are moving toward. They are funny and frustrating, sometimes distant, and often endearing. I am inspired and disappointed by them.

This year, one student touched my heart. She is a lovely girl, with large eyes, long hair, and slender limbs. Shy and nervous, she speaks—when she speaks—in a quiet voice that requires the listener to pay close attention. I knew that she was struggling with a lack of confidence, particularly early in the fall when she began working with the organization she would be doing a writing project for—the local arts council. She worried that her writing would not be adequate and she would disappoint her supervisor. As the term progressed, I read her reflective journals and was amazed at how she took herself in hand, pushed through her fear, and opened herself to the concerns of her placement community. She later gave a presentation to the class about her experience. She wanted to convey the importance of the arts in citizens' everyday lives. She started with an image of Bruce Springsteen on the screen at the front of the classroom, with these words across the image: "Artist? Musician? Life-saver?"

Then she told us a story of a teenager who had become very ill. The girl's doctors gave her three months to live unless she committed herself to a rigorous treatment protocol, one that would test her close to, or beyond, her capacity. She agreed to try; she wanted to live.

"The only thing that kept her going through those terrible weeks and months," my student said, "was the music of Bruce

Springsteen. During her daily trip to the hospital, the girl would put on her headphones, close her eyes, and draw strength and courage from his songs." She paused and I sensed us all, as a class, holding our collective breath. "She made it," she said. Another pause as she seemed to muster courage again. "That teenager was me." An audible gasp filled the room, and I struggled to keep my tears to myself.

On the second last day of the term, she came with the rest of the class, filled out my survey, engaged in our discussion, handed in her final essay, and left. She did not attend the final class, and I never got to say goodbye.

I was too little when the assaults began to understand that Friday nights were the worst. Dad could drink freely then; he didn't have to go to work the next day. Because my life was not yet regulated by the routine of school, each day seemed the same, so I was unable to anticipate the coming storms of violence. Later, my mother's lapses into fits of rage or tears and her occasional unspeakable activities in the night were even harder to predict. No matter how I tried to be good, to observe and mitigate her moods, I couldn't stop the terror and the pain. I longed, then forgot to long, for calm waters, for someone who would draw me into a safe, protected port and let me stay there.

"A woman from Samaria came to draw water. Jesus said to her, 'Give me a drink' ... The Samaritan woman said to him, 'How is it that you, a Jew, ask for a drink from me, a woman of Samaria?' ... Jesus answered her, 'If you knew the gift of God, and who it is that is saying to you, "Give me a drink," you would have asked him, and he would have given you living water.' The woman said to him, 'Sir, you have nothing to draw water with, and the well is deep. Where do you get that living water? Are you greater than our father Jacob? He gave us the well and drank from it himself, as did his sons and his livestock.' Jesus said to her, 'Everyone who drinks of this water will be thirsty again, but whoever drinks of the water that I will give him will never be thirsty again. The water that I will give him will become in him a spring of water welling up to eternal life." (John 4: 7–14, ESV)

In rural Africa, the drawers of water are women and children, mostly girls.[12] Some girls fetch and carry water rather than go to school. They collect from wells, pumps, or standpipes. Although most women walk only a short distance for water each day, some women in villages and rural areas in Kenya, for example, may walk up to twenty kilometers to fetch the day's supply.

Besides the time consumed in getting water, there are concerns about both its quality and quantity. Water systems are often haphazardly maintained because resources and expertise aren't available to replace rusting pipes and pumps. Unprotected springs or unlined wells can lead to contaminated drinking water and diseases like Guinea worm. The quantity of water available to a household directly affects its level of hygiene. The amount used for bathing, washing dishes and clothes, and other cleaning tasks is twice as much when water is readily available—in piped households or those with wells. These households are better protected against water-borne diseases; thus, the health of rural Africans depends on having an easily accessible source of clean water.

Jacinta lives in a small village in rural Kenya.[13] She is fortunate to have a tin roof rather than a thatched one, so she can collect rainwater in barrels. Although she avoids the water in the nearby stream because it attracts disease-carrying mosquitoes and tse tse flies, she has been unable to prevent mosquitoes from breeding in her standing water supply. To supplement her rainwater, she walks one and a half kilometers each day to a standpipe, waits in line with the other women and girls, and carries her burden home on her head. She and her children use the public toilets in the village. Still, she is careful with her supply, especially in the dry season, and concentrates her usage on drinking and cooking. She washes dishes every other day and bathes herself and her children only once per week. With all her care and effort, she cannot keep her children's frequent bouts of diarrhea at bay.

Jesus understood women like Jacinta. He met a Samaritan woman at a well, possibly there to draw her household's daily supply of water. He knew of her need to return to the well again and again to quench her own thirst and to sustain the life of others. His offer to her of living water that permanently satisfies thirst might have been mystifying, but it would certainly have been intriguing. And this water of which He spoke not only had the power to refresh the partaker; it could also be a source of life for others, "a spring of water gushing up to eternal life."

As I write this piece, my husband and I are at the end of a bathroom renovation. It was time to replace the chipped pink tub and deal with the lack of insulation and the mold that was beginning to grow under the paint. Because we have a small home with only one bathroom, the month-long wait for workers to get the job done was a considerable inconvenience. There were stretches of three to five days when we had no toilet. Thankfully, we live downtown in our small city and the nearest cafe is only two blocks away. Besides visits to the cafe and its facilities, we found other ways to cope. As well, for weeks we washed ourselves in water from the kitchen sink. I was fortunate to escape to my sister's home in Niagara for a week where I had exclusive use of a full bathroom. It was blissful to feel the slight sting of the shower's hot water wake and refresh my skin.

My distress at this situation tells me how little I am able to understand women like Jacinta. I have never in my life had to walk further than a nearby room to turn on a tap and get what I need. I have never worried about the quality of my drinking water. Though I know I should think about the quantity of water I use, I have never had to ration my usage except when limiting water for my garden. How can I begin to relate to the deprivation Jacinta experiences? I can't. Still, I think I know something about thirst. I was thirsty when I was a child in need of stability and care. And I was thirsty as a young woman in need of healing.

When I was in Niagara, my sister and I met our two Estonian aunts one day for coffee. They are my father's sisters, the daughters of the stern immigrants I remember from my times on the farm in my childhood. Though they are milder in temperament than their parents, there is still a thread of steel in both of these women. They are in their seventies now, intelligent, strong in their convictions, and still beautiful, with their tastefully dyed blonde hair, their slimness, and their lovely clothes. Because I live at a distance, I don't see these aunts very often, so it takes us some time to get comfortable with each other. And I always feel a bit intimidated by them, anxious not to appear unkempt in any way or display too much emotion so that I don't come close to being the embarrassment my wild, destructive parents were.

To my surprise, our conversation during this visit became increasingly warm and pleasant as we talked about our lives and work. I began to relax. Then, and I don't know quite how this happened, they began to talk about their experiences as children in Estonia during the Second World War. I heard about how my grandmother had spooked the family's only horse, made it buck and bolt, to keep it from being appropriated by occupying German soldiers. I also heard details about the family's escape from the country. My eldest aunt remembers the stormy five-night and five-day trip by boat to Sweden across the Baltic Sea. Her memory of struggling over sick and fainting passengers to reach fresh air up on deck is one of the reasons she has no wish to return to her native land.

As they spoke, I drank in their history, my history, the history my father did not live to tell me. Then I took a risk: I told them I love to hear their stories because I have what I call thirsty ears. As an auditory learner, I absorb music, song lyrics, conversation, lectures, and I remember them. But more than anything, my ears are thirsty for stories because stories make sense of the chaos I can't understand. And the stories of my family make me feel that I belong to someone, that my family has a well from which I can draw.

Often at night, when my husband and I are lying quietly together in the darkness, I ask him questions. They are a child's questions, but still I ask them, again and again. *Is everything all right? Why?* He is patient as he answers. *Yes, everything is all right. Everything is very good. Because God loves you and is taking care of you.* The answers are always the same, yet I need to hear him speak them. Again and again I go to the well. Again and again I drink. And, with time, I am satisfied.

# PART SIX

# Partnership and Home

GROWING UP, I WASN'T THE KIND OF GIRL WHO MOONED over boys or dreamed of someday getting married. I was more likely to play school than house with my friends in the basement of my home. The one crush I had on a boy in public school—an athletic boy with hazel eyes framed by thick black lashes—was mercilessly quashed. I became convinced that boys weren't interested in me: somehow I lacked the ways other girls had of winning them, or maybe I just wasn't pretty enough. In high school, my sometimes obliviousness to boys or my attraction to the wrong ones meant that I never had a boyfriend. Mostly, the lack didn't bother me, immersed as I was in school and activities, in trying to make my way in the world.

It wasn't until the end of my first year in university that I encountered someone I liked who seemed also to like me. He was in my campus Christian group, and he was also from a city very near my hometown. What drew me was his spark: he was funny and creative, with a quick, flashing grin. One evening, as we were walking through the snowy campus together, he took my hand and sent me spinning. He was patient with my initial nervousness and our relationship intensified rapidly: inexperienced as I was, I found all my boundaries dissolving. I lost myself, though I didn't know then just how lost I was already.

After three years together, just after we and our families began to think about our likely marriage, he left me abruptly. He had moved on to teacher's college, was meeting new people, and needed to grow on his own. Devastated, I staggered through the autumn of my final undergraduate year. The following spring, I discovered that he was already living with someone else, and my remaining hope of a reunion was crushed. In desperate pain, I sought help from friends and from the university chaplain. One day during this dangerous, destabilizing time, I found myself walking downtown to the shop of a friend of mine. I didn't know Ray well—we were co-leaders in our faith group—but he was kind, and I trusted him. A part-time student and owner of a picture-framing store, Ray had a calmness and warmth that felt like shelter in a storm. Like home. He took me in that day, and I stayed for life.

The beginning of our relationship was more storm than shelter for him, though. After our first weekend together, and in the months that followed, Ray was sure that he wanted to build a relationship with me. But I was still reeling and fragile, and his emotional intensity intimidated me. I would embrace his company one week and push it away the next. I needed Ray but I didn't love him, and he understood this. What I actually needed most during this time was to ground myself more deeply in my relationship with God. My summer back in my hometown and away from Ray gave me the room to find my spiritual path again. Alone in my pain and loneliness, one evening I stood at the window in my living room, watching the sun melt into the horizon beneath a sky of pink and mauve. Then words of a Psalm I knew well came to me: "Truly my soul finds rest in God; my salvation comes from him." My voice grew louder. "Truly he is my rock and my salvation; he is my fortress, I will never be shaken." (Psalm 62:1–2 NIV). I spoke these words over and over and, as they flowed from my throat and back into me, I felt myself newly anchored. Newly peaceful.

That fall, I returned to university. Complicating the situation with Ray was the presence in my life of another young man, someone I had been friends with and who had returned to school for his master's degree. I spent time with this young man while continuing to both see and resist Ray. Finally, after a year and a half of my ambivalence, Ray had enough, and he wrote me a letter to tell me so.

It was time for me to face two hard truths: I was being unfair to Ray, and I needed to make a decision about our relationship. On a clear autumn afternoon, I drove out to the country to the home of my pastor for some quiet time to think. Alone, I walked a field of straw-like, rustling grasses under a startlingly blue sky. As my feet lifted and then sank in the soft earth, I wrestled with the choice before me. Suddenly, I stopped short as the truth I needed came to me. The decision I faced was not about choosing between Ray and the other young man; it was about choosing between who God wanted for me and anyone else. At that moment, I made one of the most significant decisions of my life: I chose God's choice for me. I didn't know who that might be, but it didn't matter. I had reached solid ground.

Almost immediately, my feelings began to shift and my interest in the other young man faded. My eyes opened to see the extraordinary heart of a man I had been too afraid to appreciate. Now I could move beyond my need and embrace Ray as he was, for himself. And deeper than my awakening feelings was the new certainty in my spirit that he was the one for me. Ten months later, after an evening of sharing bread and wine together by a river, dining at an old limestone country inn, and driving back into the city, Ray and I stood together at the end of a pier in the soft summer darkness. The waves of the lake rocked their cradles of moonlight. After a time of looking out over the water, Ray turned to me and took my hands in his. Then he asked me to walk with him through the rest of our lives.

We were married in a joyful, tearful celebration seven weeks later, the morning of Thanksgiving Sunday. In a stately room of our historic city hall, filled with golden and rust-colored chrysanthemums and sheaves of wheat, we stood in the midst of our friends and family to speak our vows of commitment. Then, as we stood facing each other, our community rose up to join us. We felt hands on our heads and shoulders as they encircled us and sent prayers to lift, mingle in the air, and shower us with blessing.

# Holy Habitation

Holiness lives in the fold of an elbow, the sweep of lash
upon a cheek. Sends blood tunneling through veins
to bring life to limbs. The holiness of touch, of strength.

Holiness sparks a dulled mind to see a moment infused
with eternity. Slows a frenzied brain, ushers a return
to knowing. The holiness of sight, of understanding.

Holiness comforts a broken self, stills fear with peace.
Bathes a shame-filled soul in grace until it knows
its worth. The holiness of heart-hearing, of love.

The Holy One makes us whole until
we know ourselves as holy.

# A History of Home

What is home? Maybe it's simply the place where we reside, the place we lay our heads to sleep. For many of us, it's the best place we know; for some of us, the worst. Worst homes may barely be shelter or they may not be safe, like my childhood home. Maybe the worst homes aren't homes at all. If we're lucky, when we're older we can choose our own, choose who to be at home with. The unlucky must make or endure a home with whomever they've been cast together. We are made in homes and are shaped by homes and some of us spend our lives in search of homes where we can be remade.

When I was a graduate student in the late 1980s, I titled my master's essay "Maggie's Search for Home in *The Mill on the Floss.*" That might have been, with variations, of course, the title of my own life at that point, though I was unconscious of my need. I was aware of searching for God. But perhaps searching for God and searching for home are the same thing.

My first experience of home of the best kind came in March of 1985. I was a university student, suffering the break-up of my first serious relationship. I felt the sharp pain of rejection, loss, and dislocation; the grief left me in shambles. My friends passed me from one to the next so I wouldn't have to be by myself. But on a Friday afternoon, I found myself alone. Without a clear sense of where I was going, I wandered from my house near campus to downtown, through a small parking lot, and through the back door of the picture-framing shop of my friend Ray, a blond, bearded man a few years older than me. During our years in the faith-based campus group we both belonged to, I'd always liked Ray, enjoyed sharing ideas together as friends. He was warm and thoughtful and wise. It was good that I found my way to his shop that day. He poured me a mug of coffee and invited me to sit and hang out as long as I needed to, whether he had customers or not. I stayed talking with him for a couple of hours, and his presence calmed me, reassured me on some unconscious level that everything was all right. At the end of our visit, he invited me to his home for dinner the next day.

Upon arriving at his building, I climbed the stairs to his apartment. He ushered me in and asked me to relax in the living room while he finished making dinner. I settled myself on the old brown couch in the middle of the room, put my feet up, and looked around. Sand-colored walls and beige fabrics were soothing. A slight breeze stirred the curtains, and the room was bright with golden late afternoon light. Folk music drifted from the turntable in the corner. On one wall, Ray had hung, like art, a weathered wooden door, with its one remaining piece of glass curving in the bottom third of the frame. A rusted antique lawnmower sat in another corner. Objects discarded long ago, then found and brought home by the man currently clunking around in his kitchen. As I rested in the sunlight, carried by the sounds of music and cooking, a wave of peace entered my body and eased my bruised heart. I had a sense of being safe and cared for, of being home for the first time in my life.

I have been with Ray since then and we have been a good home for each other. Our life together has not been without challenge; we both brought brokenness into our relationship, and the healing we have needed over the years has been great and costly. But we have been joined by our desire for wholeness and our commitment to a journey of faith. In 1987 we married and moved into the house that has been home for us for more than thirty years.

This house began its life as a gift, almost 150 years ago. I know this fact because I decided recently to investigate its origins. I wanted to uncover the story of the house because it had become so dear to me, so I pored through old city directories, fire insurance plans, and census information. I discovered that, in 1870, at the age of sixty-five, William Routley and his wife, Mary, bought an empty lot a block from their house on Sydenham Street in Kingston. They then built a house for their son William K. Routley, who had been a young man when the family emigrated from England in the mid-nineteenth century. Now thirty-nine years old and employed as a shoemaker, William K., with his wife, Margaret, had a family of eight children and needed a substantial home.

It was a handsome gift, likely a financial stretch for William Senior, who was a grocer and provisioner. The house was taller and wider than the many row houses existing or soon to exist in the neighborhood. It was made of double-veneer red brick over wood instead of rough limestone, had floors laid in oak rather than soft pine planks. The three front rooms had ten-foot ceilings and were connected by wide archways. Elaborate plaster medallions graced the center of the ceilings, and a stained glass panel was set over the large window overlooking the street. It was a spacious house with a touch of grandness, speaking not only of necessity and generosity but of love and pride.

For the next ten years, William K. and Margaret's family seemed to thrive. In 1871 a school was built next door, and all the children attended except eighteen-year-old John, who had become a tobacconist in a shop on Princess Street. But William Senior's long association with the Frontenac Loan and Security Company suggests that it may have been difficult for him to hold on to the property. In 1880 he sold the house to Elizabeth Mahood who, for the next decade, rented it out to a painter, a mariner, a boiler-maker, and other working-class folk.

Aside from this ten-year period, what is striking about the house's history is the dedication of its owners. In the years that he and his family lived elsewhere, William K. Routley left shoemaking and became a tobacconist like his son John; together they established their own business on Princess Street, the main street for commercial activity in Kingston. In 1890, at fifty-nine years old, William K. reacquired the Sydenham Street house for the Routley family. After his death in 1907, the house passed to William's children, who kept it in the family until 1920, an almost fifty-year history. The Routleys' tenacity in keeping the house speaks to the gift it was in this family's life.

Longtime owners of the house were also humble people. In 1949, trucker George A. Corkey brought his new wife, Gladys, to live at the house on Sydenham Street. But he may have overreached financially. After Gladys died in 1953 and left George a young widower, he continued to live in his home but took on tenants, one couple at a time, for the next eight years. In the hands of a later owner the house was further divided so that by 1970 it consisted of three apartments, two on the second floor and one on the first, a configuration that exists today.

Our residence at the Sydenham Street house has been, for Ray and me, a gift from the beginning. In late summer of 1987, during the time we were planning our wedding, it was Ray's job to find us a home. I asked only that it be spacious, equipped with a bathtub, and filled with light. He came to the house to view number 2, the apartment on the second floor overlooking the street. It had no tub, just a tiny bathroom with a shower. It had small rooms, but a wall and ceiling had been removed, opening up the kitchen and dining area and extending the dining room ceiling to fourteen feet, to the peak of the roof. The place had the feeling of space, and light poured in through large windows on the west and south sides. With its loft bedroom in half of the former attic, it was an unusual and charming apartment, and Ray knew he had to commit to it on the spot.

We moved in two months later. For twelve years we lived in apartment 2, a place that was small and safe and quiet and lovely. Soon after our marriage began, I started to recover memories of my damaging childhood. I was gradually able to finish a master's degree, but most of the next decade I stayed at home, healing. Daytime hours I spent reading, praying, writing, going to counseling appointments, and looking after our little home; evenings we spent snuggled on the couch watching TV or sometimes visiting with friends. Ray had his own healing work to do, and he was gradually building his business, expanding into an art gallery. Humble folk doing quiet, humble things.

We were well settled in our gentle life together when the telephone rang one evening in early spring 1999. It was our landlord. He wanted to know if we would be interested in moving into apartment 1 downstairs. He would charge us no extra rent and we would have a much larger space, with a basement and a front and back yard. He would renovate the place according to our preferences; he wanted solid, long-term tenants to replace the students who were trashing the place. His offer shocked me, but I said we would consider it. And even though Ray and I were both shaken at the prospect of leaving our beloved home, I knew a ball had started rolling that I wouldn't be able to stop. It was time to move on with our lives.

Our first viewing of apartment 1 also shocked us. We didn't see the high ceilings and beautiful plaster medallions, didn't notice the stained glass over the front window. Cheap paneling covered the archway between living and dining rooms, and old, grayed carpeting partially obscured the oak floors. There was peeling linoleum in a kitchen caked black with grease and grime. The place looked dreadful, a far cry from our charming apartment upstairs and a league from the handsome house it had been. Still, we said yes and the work began. Carpeting and paneling were ripped out and the archway was opened up. The oak floors were refinished and tile replaced the linoleum in the kitchen. Deep baseboards were added to places they were missing and every room received a coat of paint.

Our move downstairs ushered in a new stage of restoration for us personally as our lives expanded. I started teaching academic writing at the university. Ray's business evolved into an art gallery, and he built an extension to provide more showing space for his artists. Our circle of friends grew, and we embraced new experiences of community life. Then, after several years in our new home, another shock came, again from our landlord. He sent us a notice to vacate in three months because he and his wife wanted to move into our apartment. Heartbroken, we began searching the city for a new place to live and moving our belongings into Ray's parents' garage. If we didn't find a suitable home in time, we could move back upstairs, but this time it would be the tiny apartment at the back. Thankfully, that move wasn't necessary. Two weeks before we had to leave, our landlord called to say that he had changed his mind; he and his wife had decided to expand their own apartment instead of moving into ours. We were relieved to be able to stay, but the dislocation had done its work: we knew we needed more stability than a life of renting could give us.

Ray and I began to explore our neighborhood for a house to buy. We wanted an old red brick house, preferably one that needed renovation and one that could give us rental income because we had no savings. We put letters in mailboxes of places we liked, hired a real estate agent, went to open houses. We came close to arranging a private deal for a house two blocks away, but one of the owners, who were separating, decided to stay. We kept looking. Then a thought struck Ray and struck him hard: the perfect home for us was the one we were already living in—the house on Sydenham Street. After that realization, Ray contacted our landlord to see if he would be willing to sell to us. He was. The transaction was private and generous on his part. Ray's mother lent us the money for a substantial down payment. A gift.

In my current life, on any given day, I return home after a morning at the university. Since my investigation of our house's history, I am now likely to walk around the neighborhood a bit first. I pause before the limestone house just around the corner where George Corkey lived in the late 1940s before he brought his new wife to live on Sydenham Street. Half a block beyond on Ordnance Street is another limestone house where George lived alone in his retirement years. As I walk these neighborhood sidewalks, I imagine Corkeys everywhere; though George and Gladys had no children, it's likely at least one of the other three brothers living in the vicinity did.

I arrive at my house, stamping the snow from my feet as I enter and then unlock the inner door. Once in our apartment I call out, as usual, "Hi, home; I'm back!" Answering words dance in my mind, "And there was much rejoicing!"

Shod of boots and coat, I pause in the dining room, which is still clad in Christmas red and gold as we like it to be until mid-February. Garlands and wreaths of berries hang in the window, frame the archway, sweep along the top of the oak bookcase, tangle in the arms of the chandelier. The dining table wears a cloth of red with cream-colored flowers and leaves of green; deep red candles sit in brass candlesticks at its center. The warm beauty cheers us during these dark midwinter days.

After lunch, I settle in at my desk for an afternoon of work. The light of late morning still lingers in my study at the back of the house. More than any other, this room is mine. The oak of the wide antique table that serves as my desk is stained golden rather than the rich browns of the furniture in the front rooms. The fabrics are lighter, too: the jute mat beneath my desk and the curtains at the windows are in shades of rose, sage, and grass green. Bookcases and natural wicker baskets fill the room. As I read the lines of my students' essays, I sometimes shift in my chair to look out the glass doors to the back yard. A chickadee swoops to the bird feeder and away. The sparrows come then and feed longer, fighting each other for a perch. Snow covers the raised bed at the back of the yard, lines the top rail of the fence above. Beyond the fence, black, feathered branches of winter trees reach into the sky. Today, as on most days, the peacefulness of my home seeps into my psyche. Sometimes the goodness of it eases out old terrors and my nights are short of sleep for a while.

But I know at these times that the peace is simply settling more deeply inside of me as restoration continues.

I turn from the view of my yard back to my work. A few hours later, evening stirs the house and brings the pleasant noises of fellow inhabitants. Our tenants come in the front door, clomp up the stairs, and begin shuffling around their apartments. Ray arrives home from the shop. I meet him at the front door, feel the whoosh of cold air as he bends to kiss me hello, his whiskers tickling my lips.

"Lovey," I exclaim after I pull back, "your ears are all red. I'll warm them up." I clap my warm palms to the sides of his head. He bears this for only an instant, though.

"I'm okay—it wasn't that bad outside," he says, not quite hiding his impatience. Mostly he's good natured when I cluck over his body, but I know he doesn't understand this preoccupation with his physical wellbeing. Today he's eager to take off his winter wear and get comfortable.

After he changes, we move around the kitchen together, putting pots on the stove, pulling out wineglasses for the dinner table. He descends to the cellar to choose a bottle from the large store of wine he's made over the years. Then he sets the table and lights all the candles, and I serve the meal. Over a long dinner, we catch up on each other's day. I tell him about some of the better essays I read that afternoon, about a concern I have with one of my teaching assistants; he is happy about the sale of a large painting. As the wine and food warm and relax us, our conversation deepens. I tell him of the insecurity I'm feeling about a friend who seems to be growing distant.

"I'm sorry," he says gently. "I know how much she means to you. But I don't think it's personal. She loves you." He pauses, then probes a little. "Is this really about your friendship, or are you maybe shifting old feelings from where they really belong?"

I always resist this kind of questioning, but he's right. He listens as I slowly allow myself to feel some of the hurt of past rejection. I talk myself out and wipe away a few tears. Then we move to the living room and nestle together on the couch. Sometimes my attention wanders from the movement and color on the television screen, and I look out the front window to the snowy street. The limestone house at the corner still has small white lights lining its windows. Snowflakes begin to drift across the path of the streetlight. Against the chill that seeps in the cracks of this old house, I snuggle in closer to Ray beneath the blanket that covers us both.

Later, one of us nudges the other awake; it's long past time for bed. I get ready and crawl in first. Then he joins me and the nightly ritual begins.

"Snorflehead," he pronounces.

"Snorflehead," I repeat, pretending offense. "That's not my name."

"Yes, it is. Dorfle Snorflehead," he says with greater confidence.

"Definitely not. That name's not in the canon," I insist, referring to the set of special nicknames I've accepted over the years.

"I know, but it's one of your revealed names. One of the million."

"Well, that's just goofy," I say, as if this behavior is new.

"No, it's not. You'll come to accept all your names one day." We both chuckle at this sweet silliness and I turn out the light.

Sometimes on a Saturday morning, after Ray has gone to work, I stay in bed with my breakfast and my book. Sunlight streams through the window and across the duvet as I nibble on a scone and turn pages. This space in my week feels like taking a deep breath and exhaling slowly. Easing open. After a couple of chapters, I lean back against the headboard and close my eyes; the palpable sense of a presence with me has drawn my attention from the pages. I breathe as I hear the tick tick of my clock and the muffled rumbling of the furnace. Another deep breath. Sometimes I speak aloud whatever is on my heart; sometimes I just listen. Always what I hear speaks to me of how loved I am. I soak in the presence of God—here in my bedroom in the quiet of morning. I am enfolded in the sweet, gentle comfort of it.

We are preparing for our annual wine-tasting party. For years, Ray and I have been winemakers, turning juice from Niagara into wine we share with friends, but we also love to explore with them other wines of the world. Before I set up the dining room, I walk around our apartment, as I sometimes do these days, imagining how the house would have been as a single-family dwelling before being divided. I see the original doorway, blocked off now, that would have been the entrance to the front room. I imagine both archways open between the sitting room, dining room, and parlor. It's harder to envision the configuration of bedrooms on the second floor, but it's certain the

Routley family would have shared just one bathroom, with its deep clawfoot tub, now the largest bathroom in the building, contained in the smaller upstairs apartment. It's not hard to imagine the house filled with the Routley parents and their many children engaged in all the rhythms of family life.

Tonight the house will be filled with friends we've chosen to share our lives with. Twelve chairs now line the perimeter of the dining room. The table in the center is laid and waiting: wineglasses gleam in the light from a single candle; a basket of bread and a jug of water sit ready for palate-cleansing between wines. Our guests begin to arrive. Deb and Dawn, who have come to many of these parties, take their places and chat with other longtime guests. Elspeth sweeps in followed by Don; their warm greetings spread through the room. At last everyone is here, and Ray and I take our places behind the table. He clears his throat for attention, smiles, and opens his arms. "Welcome, everyone, to our home and our annual wine-tasting party. Some of you have been to this party many times, some are relatively new. But we're very glad to see you all."

He talks about the place of wine in our lives as sustenance and, beyond that, as a daily celebration of beauty and communion. He encourages us to listen to wine and not just consume it, to learn how a wine speaks to us. I introduce the wine regions we'll be focusing on for the evening, their histories and geographies. Then, for those who are new to wine-tasting, we talk about observing color and clarity, about breathing in a wine's fragrance, and about holding a wine in our mouths to discern its tastes and textures. Ray begins to move around the room, pouring a small amount of the first white wine into each guest's glass. We note its perfect clarity and light straw color, inhale its floral freshness. As the evening progresses, we taste more substantial whites, then the full, rich reds everyone has been waiting for. Our cheeks flush as the wine warms us, and even the shy ones join in the chatter about body and tannin and flavor.

The formal tasting is over. People stand and stretch while Ray brings back all the wines so we can try them again. The table fills with food and music threads through the din of talk and laughter. I refill my own glass, swirl its contents, and breathe in the wine's earthy aroma. As I look around this room full of friends, I watch candlelight flicker in their faces, see the sparkle in their eyes and in the glasses they hold. The room suddenly seems more crowded than usual, and I realize that the Routleys are here, gathered around the dinner table. In the corner George and Gladys Corkey are laughing together.

And there is Ray, a smile rounding and creasing his face as he bends his head to a guest to listen. His hair and beard are whitening, now, but his heart is as wide and generous as ever. I know I've been knit together by the constancy of his love and by the Spirit that lives with us. Together, in this house, we have created a safe place for each other and, we hope, for those who pass through our doors. This steadfast man, all our friends, the former inhabitants of this house, these solid walls filled with accumulated days and nights of living and loving, have remade me. My heart, at peace, is home.

# Peeling an Egg

Sunlight falls through the kitchen window
illuminating the fine warm grain
of the cherrywood cutting board.
Above it, the egg—full and round—
is cupped and held by light's fingers
until mine take and rap it against the wood.
The caving of its shell is a small crunching sound.
I tap and roll and watch the spreading lines;
chips of white scatter across the brown surface.
Light bathes us all—hands, board, shell,
shiny albumin beneath—
softens the undoing,
the quiet,
unhurried
revealing.

# These Grapefruit Trees

These grapefruit trees have been growing in pots in my living room
since I started them from seed many years ago. They strain
toward the feeble northern light filtering through the curtains
on this gray October day. Far from the heavy moist heat
of the tropics, from the blazing sun, they are challenged
in this stark habitat. Their roots are housed in meager soil
bound by cylinders of clay. They will likely never make it
past the three feet the tallest one has reached.

Still they do their best to grow as living things will despite
being caged or displaced. They drop the leaves that have suffered
too much water, wait for dried-up branches to be pruned, send out
new shoots when the maple outside sheds its leaves
and the light inside grows stronger. I do my best for them
when I notice them drooping; I feed them water
and sometimes more. Every few years I may summon the energy
to replace their soil and give them bigger pots, or I may not.

Together we struggle toward the sun or sleep in the darkness.
We take in sustenance when we can and give what beauty we have.
We have been long companions now and I think we are patient
with each other, will care for each other in our ways while we are here.

# PART SEVEN

# Healing Years

HE FIRST FEW YEARS OF MARRIED LIFE FOR ME AND Ray were very quiet. During our honeymoon, I had begun to experience flashbacks of my childhood, particularly of my father's sexual abuse of me, so we knew it was time for me to devote myself to healing. I put my graduate studies on hold. We left the small Christian fellowship we had been part of because the ill-health we had become aware of there made the community unable to support this new stage of our journey. Ray spent his days slowly building his picture-framing business; it was all I could do to look after our home. So difficult were the memories and feelings I was recovering that I slept sometimes more than twelve hours each night. I joined a group for survivors of abuse, but after a year I realized I needed intensive therapy and found myself a counselor. My life settled into the rhythms of my healing journey: sleeping, journaling, seeing my counselor weekly, reading, resting and praying in the afternoons, puttering around my home, spending quiet evenings with Ray. This gentle, protected life enabled the painful awakening to my past to unfold.

Held in a place of rest and disengagement from the world, I began to feel the worthlessness that had driven me to achieve. Deeper, I felt the reasons for that worthlessness as I relived my experiences of my father. No longer could I escape into activity as the pain, shame, and terror of my child self rose to the surface of my psyche. This process of integration involved two essential activities: remembering and feeling. Often in the afternoons I would sit on the mission bench in our dining room, sunlight streaming through our west-facing windows, a mug of coffee in my hand. Then I would talk or write to Jesus, pouring out my pain or anger, asking my urgent questions, seeking comfort. Then the memories would come, and I would be immersed, briefly, in another terrible childhood experience of violation and betrayal.

Three years passed. One afternoon, on the couch in my living room with mug in hand, talking to Jesus, suddenly all the features of the room took on a startling clarity. I had the sense of another presence. Although my father had died twenty-five years earlier, I knew beyond a doubt that he was sitting in the chair across from me, in the green cushioned rocker that had once belonged to him. He was, of course, invisible to me, but somehow I knew that his head was bowed in shame. I began to speak to him. I didn't talk about his abuse of me because we seemed now to share an understanding of that tortured part of our history. Instead I told him anything and everything that was on my heart, as a daughter would to a father who was sober and listening. I said I wished we had come to know each other while he was alive because I thought we might have liked each other. I wished he had been around and able to help me and my sister with our troubled mother.

I didn't sense my father responding; he was there only to listen. But later that day, when I was up in the loft of our apartment making the bed, I felt his presence again. I stopped what I was doing to pay attention. This time I heard "I'm sorry. I'm sorry." Then, suddenly, a wave of sweetness and peace flooded my being. I stood still as the beauty and wonder and comfort of it moved through me. When it was over, I understood what the experience meant. I had forgiven my father. This stage of my healing journey was over.

That fall I was able to finish my studies and graduated with my master's degree. But rather than emerging from my home to take my place in the world, I entered a longer, more difficult stage of healing: facing my history with my mother. The memories grew darker and more horrifying as I slogged through reliving experiences I had forgotten. Experiences of tirades of tears and rage. Of being emotionally attacked and shamed. Of being subjected to black, violent rituals in the night.

Through the next years, terror and nightmares often robbed me of sleep. I learned how to release great waves of sadness by kneeling on my bed with my face buried in a pillow to muffle the sound, opening myself up and howling. Because of my relationship with God, I knew there was a place for all my pain and fear to go. I pictured taking these feelings to Jesus on the cross and laying them at His feet. I understood that He died in order to take them to Himself, to absorb them, so when I felt and released these feelings to Him, I knew they were gone for good.

During this time, my mother herself had come back into my life. Years earlier, my sister and I had discovered that she was living with relatives in Saskatchewan. I had contacted her and urged her to come back to Ontario, to the town where I now lived. I had thought my Christian fellowship group could help her find her way to healing. She came, but to my dismay she was as violent and unstable as ever, still addicted to alcohol and resistant to help. Fortunately, she was able to find a partner, marry, and settle into a new life, just before I married Ray.

But my mother and her husband, both heavy drinkers, soon began to spiral into relationship storms and financial difficulty. They sold his house and moved into a mobile home outside the city. It was early in my marriage and healing process; I was just beginning to recover memories of my past with my mother and found myself entirely unable to deal with her in the present. One winter day I received a phone call from the manager of a trailer park in Florida where my mother and her husband were spending several months. The woman urged me to come and get them because they had careened in their van through others' sites, damaging some property. I told her that no, I couldn't help. I had had enough. My mother continued to live near my city until her death eleven years later, but I never saw her again.

Emotionally free of my father and out of relationship with my mother, I was able to sink deeply into the healing process. Healing during these long years of remembering happened through what I came to know as a holy exchange. When a memory, a difficult feeling, or a lie about myself or the world arose, I would take it as an offering to the throne of God, the seat of mercy. The book of Isaiah speaks of the exchange: God promises "to grant to those who mourn in Zion—to give them a beautiful headdress instead of ashes, the oil of gladness instead of mourning, the garment of praise instead of a faint spirit." (Isaiah 61:3 ESV). My bundle of ashes might be my tendency to control things, a tendency that was crippling my life; it might be my fear of chaos. Whatever it was, I gave it up to God and let it go. As God took my bundle, I would often experience a gradual or sudden release of fear, anger, or pain as these emotions washed from me.

What I received in return was sometimes an immediate or usually more gradual lightness of being and an expanding capacity for joy. I gained the sense of becoming more solid as the daily nurturing love I experienced with Ray, with my counselor, and with others, and the care I was extending to myself, slowly established a new foundation. I came to know myself as loved and valued rather than worthless and abandoned. As my mind cleared of memory and the tangle of lies that had accompanied my experiences, I was given flashes of truth. And I received an answer to the deepest question of my heart—where was God was during the worst moments of my childhood?

One afternoon, I found myself remembering the Good Friday night of terror in my childhood back yard and all that happened there. Then I was given a picture of where Jesus was when that group of black-robed observants performed their diabolical ritual: Jesus was on the cross, dying. He was dying for the innocents suffering the experience; he was also dying for the perpetrators. His death meant that, no matter the depth of the damage to all of us, none of us is beyond healing. He could take—was taking—all of our pain upon Himself to open a way to restoration for each person caught in that devastation.

Some months later, as I continued to make my way through this memory, I received another image of Jesus in that back yard. This time I saw the resurrected Jesus, radiant and shining. I knew then that Jesus had gone beneath the worst of what humans do to each other, beneath the evil that they sometimes call into their midst. He broke the power of that evil to conquer us in the end. These images I received, these gifts of insight, continued the solidifying work in my psyche and spirit.

Ray and I reached our tenth anniversary, and it was time for us to reflect on the path we had chosen. I was still healing at home and Ray was continuing to build his small business, which was prospering. Our lives were filled with companions who understood and supported our journey. But we knew that some were wondering at the length and intensity of it. That autumn, we walked together in a wood just outside our city. Hand in hand, we talked and sought guidance from God. As we considered the long years of healing, we saw that God had been faithful: He had provided the understanding we needed to navigate the territory of memory, the strength to do the emotional work, and the support we needed to sustain our lives. And the journey was taking both of us into increasing wholeness.

That day, our determination to follow God on the unusual journey He was leading us on grew stronger.

That conviction was necessary to see us through the next two years. My memory work shifted to a different, earlier childhood experience of ritual abuse. Reliving this experience meant days of despair and darkness so deep that sometimes being alone was dangerous. But we knew the way through, and God held me through the cleansing of this part of my past.

Then, suddenly, life opened up, expanded. We moved from our small safe home to a much larger apartment downstairs in the old house we were living in. My growing strength enabled me to start working, first as a freelance editor and then as a teaching assistant at the university. My therapy sessions with my counselor ended. From the foundation of loving relationship that had been established within me—with myself, with God, with Ray and others—I could now move out into the world.

# Trinity Prayer

You who come on the gentle wind
that lifts my hair and strokes my weary body,
you of the warming sun
that softens the hard pain I keep within

lay me in the cradle of your peace,
fill with love the yawning hollows of my soul,
mend the feeble shreds of tattered trust
until my heart is whole.

You who walk on water, still,
with quiet, dancing feet of lilting light,
you of the singing air
that breathes into my spirit and my ear
the pure clear song of wild eternity

call me now to join you in your joy,
wash my mind with truth and set it free,
cleanse it of its paths of brokenness
until I feel the living waves
beneath my feet.

You who tremble in every cell
and sway the ancient clans of towering trees,
you of the shifting earth,
of sky that opens wide its mouth of blue
and blows a wakening breath

touch my spirit, loose its latent spark,
stir the song of love that lives in me,
let it rise through places numbed or mute
until I am a singer
and a song.

# The Life of Wine

My two companions—my sister Marianne and my friend Megan—are as lively as the most effervescent sparkling wine. Today, though, we are tasting still wines at a winery in Prince Edward County, the island wine region in southeastern Ontario.

The winemaker, James, pours a golden liquid into our glasses. A filmmaker by profession, he is tall and lanky with thick graying hair and black-framed glasses, and he seems amused by our excitement. The smooth, rich nuttiness of the chardonnay warms us to effusiveness. Megan's voice grows louder. She sends questions at James like a puppy shaking a spray of drops into the sunlight. Aged how long? In what type of oak? Malolactic fermentation?

We move on to two bottles of pinot noir. Marianne's eyes radiate pleasure and her brow crinkles as she concentrates on identifying flavors. Raspberry? Cherry? A hint of spice? Our cheeks flush and our tongues loosen. We tell James about the wine courses that Marianne is taking and about the small vineyard that my husband and I are intending to plant several kilometers from here. Our clear joy in this moment (my eyes must be shining too) and the wine knowledge we exhibit seem to nudge James beyond his usual hospitableness. He invites us to follow him for an experiment. We walk behind him out of the tasting house down a muddy lane through a vineyard and in the side door of a large weathered barn. We are in a barrel room.

James leads us between two rows to a barrel near the end. He pulls out the stopper, draws some wine, and partially fills a glass. Then he passes the glass to us for our first taste. This wine is young, simple, and fruity, and we admire its cheerfulness. Then we move up the row and drink from a different barrel. We taste pinot noir again, but this time the flavors are more complex and the wine seems more weighty.

James introduces us to pinot noir from seven different barrels. All of them are from the same vintage; all have been aged for the same amount of time in French oak. As we sip the wine from the last barrel, he explains:

The differences in the wines from the different barrels come from the characteristics of the clones I've chosen for each vineyard, from the location of the vines, and from the soil in which the grapes grew. Grapes from certain rows may have received slightly different levels of moisture or heat or been exposed to different airflow patterns than those from only several rows away. Maybe the soil has a bit more sand, loam, or clay in particular parts of the vineyard than in others. The grapes and the wine reflect their terroir, as the wine world calls it.

We are honored to taste these wines, so distinct from each other, in their infancy, so we try to listen and respond to them carefully. We want to give James something back, offer meaningful observations, but our words fumble from us. Maybe our best response is to simply be still and linger in this experience, to let ourselves be carried along in the currents of sensation and companionship. Maybe all James needs are witnesses, not words. In the end we smile, murmur our gratitude, and shake hands with him, all of us filled to the brim.

## Step 1: Harvesting and Crushing

The team of vineyard manager, winemaker, and proprietor hovers and tastes and waits until the precise time arrives for harvest. The grapes are at the perfect stage of ripeness for picking when the sugar level is just right and the flavors clearly show the characteristics of the variety. Then the vineyard workers are called in to cut the clusters from the vines and haul the bins of fruit to the winery for careful sorting.

Immediately after sorting, the grapes are dumped into a huge mechanical crusher that breaks their skins and reduces them to must—a mixture of juice, pulp, seeds, and skins. Juice that is to become red wine is then left to absorb the color, flavors, and tannins of the skins during the next step in the process—fermentation.

As a young woman, alone and desperate, I place my life in the hands of God. Then I leave home for school: a vine transplanted into good ground. Faith, like roots, deepens. A jumble of housemates, a community, teachers—the warming sun. Learning. Growing strong. The vinedresser tends the vine.

The time comes. My first love ends: the cutting, the crushing. My life splits open; shredded skins of the present mix with the broken pulp of my past. Maceration.

It is a cool May day in the County, but the breeze hints at the warm weather coming. Friends and family continue to arrive at this patch of land several miles south of Picton, Ontario. Ray's brother Curtis has agreed to let us use a small square of the most inhospitable ground on his property for a vineyard—soil that only grapes can flourish in. Today the field sits open to the sun, earth newly tilled to loose clumps and skimmed with flickering shadows as thin clouds pass overhead. It is planting day.

More cars bump along the lane that borders the field and stop beside our growing group: Marianne and Ed from Niagara; Ray's parents, elderly now; a close friend and her dog; a couple and their teenaged son. One young friend has brought her mother, who seems too fragile for the work ahead, her woolen cap not quite hiding a new baldness. We now cluster in twos and threes, chattering, all of us clad in jeans and jackets, with shovels in hand and an eagerness to begin. Ray calls us together into a circle for a blessing. And though we have differing experiences of faith, we clasp hands anyway and join our hearts in the task before us and the goodness of the land and the sky and each other. Then we set to work.

Deb, Dawn, and their daughters—all strong women—move to dig the riesling row where the soil is the rockiest. Irwin, Sue, and Jesse start the chardonnay row next to it. Helen and I decide to plant the cabernet franc row along the edge where the topsoil is deepest. We sink our spades in the ground four feet apart, trying to center our holes under the string that runs from one end of the field to the other. This digging is hard work. Though the ground has been tilled, it is rocky; sometimes we have to shimmy our shovels under large chunks of limestone, push down on the handles, and try to hoist the rocks up and out. Sometimes we hit a solid shelf of rock. Then we have to call one of the men working the pickaxes to come and break it up.

After we have dug the holes, we walk up our row to one of several buckets and lift out plants—pieces of vine about eight inches long with a wax-covered graft in the middle and a spray of long roots at the end. We trim the roots and fan them out as we place a plant at the bottom of each hole. Then we shovel the dirt back in, burying the vine to an inch below the graft. I murmur encouragement to each one.

We break to share a meal together, easing our stiffening limbs into chairs set up near the cabin and raising glasses to toast our efforts. Many of the folks here are strangers to each other, but we have labored hard together, drawn the same clean air into our working lungs and muscles, blistered our hands, and made a vineyard. A vineyard Ray names for a Bruce Cockburn song and for this gathering, this "Festival of Friends."

## Step 2: Fermentation

Fermentation begins when the winemaker introduces a chosen strain of yeast into the must to kill off wild yeasts and control the process. The yeast converts the sugar in the must to carbon dioxide and alcohol. Fermentation continues until a dry red wine is produced, with no residual sugar, a process of ten days to a month or more.

The next stage and I am led again. The chosen yeast is love: a new partner and a home together. Safety. Rest. Quiet. My mind opens to memory, the foment of truth. Remembering, remembering. A walk through the shadows of the past, accompanied by a sage, enfolded by the Spirit. The Winemaker hovers. Love mingles with pain, releases it. A process of years.

I arrive home from a weekend away to find Ray looking the worse for wear. He has a badly sunburned neck and a nagging cough. He seems happy, though, as he relates the details of his days of work in the vineyard.

The work began on Saturday when he arrived at the vineyard with the early morning sun, Fist-Bump Ed in the passenger seat of the car and a case of beer in the back. Grizzled and sunburned, Fist-Bump is a well-known character in the county who looks a decade older than his forty years. But Ray and Curtis knew how hard he could work in the twenty minutes between his breaks for cigarettes and tallboys. Curtis was waiting for them with the auger, pounder, and metal posts that had been delivered in advance. The vines were in their second year, so it was time to train them up to wires strung between the posts. That day Ray, Curtis, and Fist-Bump planned to pound in the metal posts and drill the holes for the cedar ones they'd drive in the next day at the end of the rows.

The men set to work on the first row, banging a post into the ground a foot deep every fifteen feet, for four metal posts per row. It was jarring work. In some places, they couldn't force their way through the solid limestone shelf. They needed a better pounder. Ray and Fist-Bump headed off to get the equipment and another case of beer.

After all the posts were in place, the men faced an even bigger challenge: drilling holes for the cedar posts, fourteen in all. It was midafternoon and they were aching and exhausted from all the pounding. Ray was trying to ignore the poison ivy rash creeping up his left shin and the chigger bites screaming for scratching. The three together gripped the auger set to drill the first hole. Fist-Bump got it started, and the rough buzz filled their ears. They struggled to hold it steady as it hit roots and rocks and slowly sank into the earth. This hole had to be cut on the diagonal, and it had to be two feet deep. Finally, the auger had gone deep enough, and the men took a break before moving on to the next row.

Three holes later, the auger slammed into solid rock, jerked Curtis off his feet, and flung him to the ground. Time for another break. Two holes further along, Ray erupted in a spasm of coughing from inhaling the fumes the auger was spewing in his face. It was time to call it a day. Half of the holes were dug for the posts, and Fist-Bump would return the next day to help finish the job. Before he and Ray turned to go, they all surveyed what they had done. Neat lines of metal posts stood straight against a sky turning golden in the early evening. Soon all the holes would be dug and wooden posts would slant at the end of the rows. This little vineyard was taking shape. Ray saw a slight smile cross Fist-Bump's lined and ruddy face as he raised his right hand to Curtis and Ray, gave their knuckles a clumsy knock, and lowered himself into the car.

"It was a good day in the end," Ray told me with a rueful smile. "And then there was Sunday."

## Step 3: Clarification

During the clarification stage, the new wine is separated from the solids, or pomace. The winemaker racks or siphons the wine from one tank to another, leaving the pomace at the bottom of the fermenting tank. For further clarification, the wine may be filtered or fined. In fining, the winemaker adds a substance such as egg white or clay to the wine; this substance attaches to dead yeast cells and other unwanted solids and draws them to the bottom of the tank. The clarified wine is then racked into another vessel, ready for the next stage in the process.

The winemaker purifies the wine: lies, ghosts are left behind as the healing continues. Sleep-steeped mornings still follow dark nights, but the darkness is not so deep. My mind and body are siphoned from shame, lifted from fear. Reading, writing, praying on the couch in the slant of afternoon sunlight. Into a growing radiance.

The parking lot behind the gallery, hemmed in on two sides by limestone walls and at the rear by the fire hall, is a good, sheltered place for pressing. It is a late November day, with a light covering of snow on the gravel of the lot. Though Ray and I are in toques and gloves, we're glad to be protected from the wind.

Our own vines are still too young to produce a harvest, so today we're pressing wine made from juice and must we fetched from Donna and David Lailey in Niagara-on-the-Lake almost a month ago. The juice has now fermented and soaked in the flavors of red grape seeds and skins. Before us today are nine pails of young wine: gamay, pinot noir, and cabernet franc.

The large glass carboys, rinsed and sterilized, stand waiting in a gleaming line in the sun. We've assembled the wooden cage and iron platform of the basket press. Ray starts to pour gamay from the first pail into the press. The young wine runs in a purple stream into the cage and through the slats, then descends in a rush from the spout of the platform into the small bucket beneath. When that bucket is full, we divide this free-run juice between two waiting carboys. As we continue to pour from the big pail, the basket fills with fermented skins until it is almost full. We work in a quiet, focused way, speaking only through the rhythms of our bodies as we lift and swing and pour and pass pails from one of us to the other.

The headiness of the wine fills my nostrils and softens the sharpness of the winter air. Our toques and gloves are off. I plunge my hands into the wet slipperiness of the skins in the press and push down, forcing more juice between the slats. This is the best part of the day, when my hands are sunk deep in wine and must. I pull them out and delight in my stained skin, lined almost black in the creases. I lift my hands to Ray with a grin. They make me feel more connected, somehow, than I normally do in my indoor world of words.

Now it is time for the full press. Ray places wooden blocks over the skins in the basket and screws the iron cap over them. Then he fits the end of a pole into an opening in the cap and begins to circle the pole around the press, winding down. The wine runs through the slats again. As it gets more difficult to turn, we begin to push the pole together, each in a semi-circle toward the other. We push hard to extract the last concentrated drops of juice. When all of the wine has dripped into the small bucket, we remove the cap and blocks from the basket and shake the cake of pressed skins into an empty pail.

We repeat this process with the rest of the wine until the light starts to drain from the sky and cold creeps beneath our clothes. We find our gloves and hats. Then we stand back to admire the line of full jars, glowing ruby red to inky purple in the last light of day.

## Step 4: Aging and Bottling

Aging and bottling comprise the final stage of the winemaking process. The wine is racked into large oak barrels or small barriques. As it rests for months or even years in barrel, the wine absorbs additional flavors from the wood; American oak often imparts vanilla notes while French oak suggests butterscotch flavors in a finished wine. The wine also becomes more concentrated through very slow evaporation. Finally, the winemaker determines that the desired flavor profile and balance have been reached. Then begins the process of siphoning the wine into bottles, capping or corking them, and shipping the finished cases to market.

Life expands with a growing strength to admit the here and now. The added flavor of work, sitting together with a student in a small room, bent over a piece of writing. The filling out, the rounding.

Then we're led again, this time to a new home. Evenings spent in the back yard with friends, clinking glasses, laughing. A life of love, a love of life, shared now with others. Communion. Gratitude to the winemaker for a steady and compassionate hand.

We are in the barrel room at Lailey Vineyard in Niagara-on-the-Lake. Outside the August sun shines hot, but this room is dim and cool. Heavy oak casks line the wall nearest us. We face each other in a circle of seven: the wine-maker Derek Barnett and his assistant Colin, Donna and David Lailey, Ray, Marianne, and me. We are sipping pinot noir, letting the silky liquid slide over our tongues and fill our cheeks, feeling its warmth as it moves down our throats and through our bodies. We try to listen to the wine's notes and nuances, to find words that describe the cherry brightness and delicate charm we are tasting together.

Though we all make wine for different reasons, as a hobby or a profession, we share the richness it brings us. We sip and talk, about wine regions, about the unique and sometimes challenging characteristics of Ontario wine. But what we don't express is what we all know: the soil of vineyards giving way under our feet, the translucent green of sunlit grapes, the musky fragrance of ripe fruit in the cool October air. Hands stained purple-black from immersion in the crushed skins and juice of red grapes. The yeasty pungence of fermenting must filling our nostrils. The froth of wine streaming through troughs and tubes into bottles waiting to receive it. As we hold our glasses this afternoon in the barrel room, we hold, too, in that space within our circle, the goodness of wine and life shared together, swirling and fragrant and holy.

# PART EIGHT

# Work, Writing, and Sisterhood

IN JANUARY OF 2000, I WANDERED THROUGH THE BASEMENT of a large building on campus, at last finding and climbing the few stairs to the continuing education office. I was starting a position as a teaching assistant for a correspondence writing course, and I was terrified. Not having been a TA as a graduate student, I had no idea how to mark the thirty essays I was about to retrieve. But I had the wherewithal to reassure myself: "In a few months, weeks even, this process will be familiar, even comfortable." Eight months later, I just as anxiously walked the stone path to the university's Writing Center, a small yellow house at the edge of campus, to begin my first shift tutoring students. I was nervous because I was an inexperienced thirty-eight-year-old newly returning to the workplace after a twelve-year hiatus I could fully explain to almost no one. And I was coming back to a campus where I felt I had largely limped through my degrees, so I was uncertain about being qualified to teach there. The only thing I could do to calm myself was invite God to walk before and beside me into this place and bless my work.

And my new life was blessed indeed. The Writing Center, with its tutoring program and writing courses, eased me into the world of work remarkably gently. I could teach part-time and gradually add shifts or courses as my strength grew. As well, the director of the center, an amiable English professor who brought his dog to his office every day, had a knack for hiring sensitive, creative folk who were passionate about supporting student writing. He built the kind of collegial community that gave us all the environment we needed to learn to teach well.

Through the years, some of the students I worked with at the center became regulars. Jennifer, a global development studies major, was possibly the brightest student I ever worked with. Because of her skill in essay writing and the depth of her research and insight, I was sure she didn't need my writing advice; still, she sought me out for confidence-building encouragement as she struggled through exhaustion to the conclusion of a project. One evening in her tiny apartment, where we had permission to conduct a few of our sessions, she read aloud to me one of her final essays. Her black cat sprawled across the papers on the kitchen table, oblivious to the power of the ideas filling the room. But I was honored to listen and learn from this gifted, idealistic young woman, as I was honored to accompany so many students through their studies.

My personal healing work continued, but my energy increasingly shifted to this new life outside my home. In my work, I advanced from teaching assistantships to instructing my own courses, from tutoring at the Writing Center to training and mentoring other tutors. Sometimes I struggled emotionally: with the split between my personal and professional lives, between my present and my past. When I felt overwhelmed by my responsibilities or by the flood of feeling that still sometimes arose from old wounds, I longed to be able to tell my supervisors where I had come from. Sometimes the weight of work combined with the intensity of the healing process seemed unmanageable. But I found myself growing both stronger and freer with time, and I came to trust that each term's load would be just right for me, because it always was. Often I was reminded of this promise: "Come to me, all who labor and are heavy laden, and I will give you rest. Take my yoke upon you, and learn from me, for I am gentle and lowly in heart, and you will find rest for your souls." (Matthew 11: 28–29 ESV) That yoke of good work was a gift from the One who was healing me.

In my mid-forties, with reading and writing at the center of my professional and personal lives, I experienced an unexpected, radical shift in vision. It was a sunny summer day and I was in my back yard, engrossed in a novel with my feet up on a nearby chair and overhead branches casting moving shadows on the pages. Suddenly the words seemed to blur before my eyes, but I soon realized that there was no physical failure in my ability to see. My vision had simply changed, and I was noticing things I hadn't been aware of before: the sound of the writer's voice, the details of description, the pacing and purpose of the passages. Later I understood this shift; I had begun to read as a writer.

Soon after, writers began crowding into my life, and a few became friends. One of them challenged me to attend a summer short fiction writing class. Though my instinct was to be wary of new challenges, her words sounded a gong in my spirit, a call to a new adventure I couldn't ignore. So I wrote my first short story and set out for an unfamiliar university in a big city several hours from my home. Despite my trepidation, the first morning of class I was struck with the sense of being in the right place at the right time. After this experience, more stories followed, poems and reflective pieces, too, in a flow that has continued. Other writing supports have come as well: retreats, writing groups, and wise readers who have understood my heart and mind and helped me find my voice; the great gift of a writing studio to come to every week. In becoming a writer, I have found that I can draw on a capacity developed through the long years of healing: an ability to listen. I listen for the silent voice of the Spirit who teaches me and helps me to write true things, to sing through the middle of a note.

My closest companion on my healing and creative journey, besides Ray, has been my sister. It is a joy to read to her what I have written because she knows me so well, and she always hears the false or missing note. She is also always eager to listen to me talk about the steps I'm taking toward wellness, although her path has been very different from mine. Hers is not the way of remembering, partly because she has been able to access only fragments of memory from the years before she was nine years old. Her psyche might be protecting her from being overwhelmed by the truth. What she has been left with is dark impressions, a persistent anxiety, and an occasional rise of intense feeling—the hurt of deep deprivation. Though she was not abused directly by our parents, she was the lost sister, the forgotten one, the silent witness. Her path to wellness has been fueled by her determination to become strong and independent; essential to her emerging and solidifying personhood has been the freedom to find her own way. She has forged a career in elementary school teaching and a partnership with an older man, both of which have given her the challenge and room she has needed to grow.

Possibly because she grew up feeling forgotten and neglected,

Marianne has embraced family in a way that I haven't. I left our mother and extended family behind in order to heal and created a family of friends, while she stayed in relationship with our mother. After our mother died, Marianne cared for our mother's husband, her stepfather, the only person in her life who has come close to being a father. Since his passing, she has become more involved with our two elderly aunts, who now rely on her for help. Sometimes her need to tend to them, as she tended to our mother and her husband before them, has made me feel that she is neglecting our relationship or taking it for granted; there have been times during our brief visits when she has gone off to shop for an aunt or help in a garden. This feeling is fading with time, though. Despite the occasional strain we feel when each of us wants her own way, we know deep in our bones the power of our sister bond. The times we feel alienated from each other are short because we confront whatever is in the way of being in relationship. Usually, she is the one who hears the hurt in my voice and calls me out to hash things through. During the decades of our lives, as people and responsibilities have come, as well as changes and losses, we have continued to walk together—out of the damage of our childhood and into the wholeness that is our hearts' hope.

# Prairie Morning

My sister has never seen such wide
prairie spaces, been this close to clouds.
But she loves light-filled landscapes,
bold sunflowers, bright blue skies,
the friendliness of sunshine that radiates
like her. She is with me here.

I have lost her from time to time.
During recent dinner party talk,
she spoke of childhood hiding places—
up the telephone pole (how did she
get up there?), squeezed in a drawer
of the captain's bed—I didn't know
she was missing. Worst, shadowy, grown-up
figures in the backyard on a black night
and her disappearing into the shed.
Later, I left for school and left her behind.

We forgive each other our absences,
our misguided loyalties, because we must.
We are essential to each other as breath,
the strong prairie winds that sweep the sky clean,
the winds that move in us, blowing in strength,
blowing out lies, carrying us into that bright sunshine.

# Flying Home

At last. The plane rolls into position on the runway and starts to accelerate. After a long, frustrating wait at the airport, we're finally on our way. I risk a glance at Marianne, but her face is already buried in her book, one of those Ian Stewart novels she can't get enough of. Normally we'd grin at each other as the plane picked up speed, rambled and roared, and lifted into the air. As sisters, we've always loved flying. But now I close my eyes as I'm pressed into my chair by the plane's forward thrust. When I open them again, I stare out the window at the rows of whitewashed buildings and red tile roofs shrinking as we ascend. I don't try another glance at Marianne.

Then the seatbelt light goes off and the captain's voice fills the cabin. "Welcome aboard Flight 540 direct from Lisbon to Toronto. Our travel time today should be five hours, forty minutes, landing at 3:15 local time." An attendant at the top of our aisle begins his demonstration of emergency procedures, and I survey the other passengers. With their dark hair and eyes, many appear to be Portuguese, families going to Canada to visit or returning home after visiting relatives in Portugal. Marianne and I stand out as tourists, but it comforts me to be surrounded by chattering children, parents, and grandparents, like we're in the midst of a big warm family.

The silence between Marianne and me is entrenched, but she seems unconcerned. Maybe she thinks her barely audible "Sorry, Lori" was enough to dismiss the whole fiasco at the airport, and she is leaving me to get over it. I still see her sauntering toward me as I wait in a seating area with all our luggage. Sauntering after dawdling in the duty-free shopping area, making us late at the checkpoint we hadn't anticipated. I see again the long line of anxious passengers who had also miscalculated, passengers who stood between us and reaching our gate in time for our flight.

I let myself feel the resentment I have kept to myself on this trip. My face is turned toward the window, but I'm back in Pinhao, at the top of the stairs leading to the Quinta Do Bomfim winery buildings, looking back toward the village streets for her. The group behind me is starting the tour, but still there is no sign of her. Finally, she comes into view, strolling along at her usual leisurely pace despite me calling her name and urging her to hurry. We join the group partway into the tour, and I have trouble looking at her for a while.

What happened after that was probably the worst thing, though. We had slowly warmed to each other again and were sitting on the deck of the winery, sipping samples and listening to the server describe the wines. The Douro River sparkled beneath us and sent a breeze to cool our skin. This was what we had come for: a chance to enjoy the wine we loved and share an adventure together. We nattered with the server as the wines flushed us with good feeling. We then became aware of three women at a nearby table who were speaking English. We sent a friendly comment their way and soon we were a group, conversing about the wines and sharing our experiences as travelers. Marianne connected particularly with a woman named Ilka, a tanned, healthy-looking teacher from Minnesota with ultra-short hair and round wire glasses. Marianne learned that Ilka was traveling alone and invited her to come and stay at our quinta with us, even though Ilka had a room booked in town. Marianne's invitation meant that Ilka was with us for a whole day in the meager seven days that Marianne and I had together.

After the winery tour, Marianne, Ilka and I drove back to our quinta, which was another winery but with the benefit of a small inn. We then took Ilka to dinner that evening. As we traveled the river road to Regua in the fading light, I think Marianne and I both realized what we were in for. Ilka told us about her recent divorce and her return to her parents' farm, about the loss of her teaching job and the injustices of the American education system. As she went on, Marianne tried to interject here and there with a detail about our lives, but I quickly gave up and sat in defeated silence. Dinner was no better. We went to the same traditional Portuguese restaurant that Marianne and I had been to the night before and had the same jovial, middle-aged man as a server whom we communicated with by pointing, nodding, and smiling. But Ilka continued to talk, loudly and embarrassingly, through the whole meal. Marianne and I exchanged a couple of exasperated looks, but at a certain point I stopped listening and responding and left the burden of the conversation to her. I concentrated on tasting more fully the roasted cod and potatoes on my plate, on observing more closely the Portuguese families gathered here for their evening meal, and on joking with the French couple at the next table. And I appreciated the irony of the cliché we made: two overly polite Canadian women dominated by a loud American.

Dinner over at last, we returned to the quinta. Ilka wanted to drink together, but Marianne and I retreated to our suite. I was eager to debrief the experience with Marianne, but she said she needed some down time and went up to her loft to read. For a while I tried to read in bed, but it was impossible to concentrate. I felt that Marianne had left me for a stranger whom, for some reason, she had decided to help. The next morning, Ilka was with us for breakfast and later the quinta's winery tour. I avoided her and Marianne, miserable in my disconnection from my sister.

Now as I look out the window I don't see the plain of white clouds beneath us because bitterness spreads in my mind. Marianne and I conceived of this trip to celebrate our relationship, two sisters free at last from the burden of our parents. I thought she would finally be fully with me, no longer placating our dangerous mother or nursing our mother's failing husband. Through our adulthood and my long estrangement from our mother and Otto, I kept waiting for her to choose me, to come back, to return to the desperate intimacy of our early childhood when we were each other's only safety.

But she never did choose me, and now I begin to understand that she never will. More than she needs to be with me, she needs to rescue someone else, to take care of someone weaker than herself or whom she perceives to be the weaker.

Friends back home—well, acquaintances, really, because friends understand—gave me an odd look when I let it slip that this first sister trip of ours was to celebrate finally being free of parents. I forget sometimes that people usually mourn the deaths of their parents and miss them when they are gone. When our father died just before my thirteenth birthday, I felt nothing but relief—well, relief mixed with an awareness that I was somehow in the middle of a tragedy. There would be no more anxious Sundays with a drunken father, inebriated maybe because he couldn't face us sober knowing what he had done when we were little. Maybe the guilt was too much for him in the end.

Our mother made it decades past him, to her late sixties. She and her second husband managed to stop drinking and lead a relatively tranquil retired life. This quiet period was too late for me, though. I had parted with them five years before, after being called one too many times by police wanting me to get them under control. After almost ten years of estrangement, a couple of years before she died, I attempted to reconcile with her. I wrote her letters recalling the best of the past, the fun in my childhood. The pets and friends filling the house, treasure hunts on birthdays. Eating popcorn and snuggling under the blue blanket, watching *The Waltons*. I then proposed that we meet with a mediator present, but I insisted on one condition of my involvement in this process: that we agree to face together the truth of our shared past. Then I laid out, in another letter, what I remembered from those dark, dark early years as a family. What she and Dad had done. Marianne was visiting her when that last letter arrived and the screaming began—my sister once again the witness to chaos. The possibility of my reconciling with my mother dissolved in her threats to hire a lawyer and sue me. That reaction seems laughable now, and it was even then, but it was the final break between us.

I glance over at Marianne, her head still lowered in her book, and I remember those curls when they were softer and lighter. Springier, sometimes when she was a small child matted with the honey that she loved. How hard I tried to prevent her from being damaged as I was. I was too young to know that simply witnessing everything was enough to infect all her cells with fear.

Maybe it was that fear that kept Marianne attached to our mother through all the years of our mother's life. I don't know, maybe it was more than that. Need, maybe. Compassion, even, later on. Still, I know that Marianne was as relieved when our mother died as I was when our father took his life. Now Otto is gone, and Marianne and I are enjoying our freedom. But I don't know how to find my way back to her. At home, Ray and I sit down together and hash things out, no matter how long it takes or how hard the process is. I resist these talks sometimes, but they always take us to a better, clearer place. I sense now, though, that Marianne and I won't be able to work through our differences, the reasons for the friction between us on our trip. She seems compelled sometimes to jump into circumstances without considering all those involved. I am a sensitive creature prone to getting bruised by her actions, but I understand now, in a way that I never have before, that I have to accept her as she is.

As she is. I turn to her again and watch her for a little while, noting the golden glints in her chestnut hair and the way her thick lashes are lowered with her downward gaze. She must feel my eyes on her because she finally lifts her head.

"Hey, Mare," I say gently. "How's the book going?"

"It's good," she says. "How long have we been flying?"

"About forty-five minutes or so. I think I'm going to look through my photos."

"Good idea," she says. "I will too." She reaches down and riffles through her purse, searching for her phone, as I dig in my bag for my camera. An image lights the screen in front of me.

"My pictures start with our walk near the hotel in Nazare." I show her a photo of the pine woods we saw with the bright green succulent shrubs at the base of the trees. "Too bad we don't have pictures of our arrival or our drive north."

"Too bad!" She laughs. "I'd like to forget that first part. It was such a hassle renting the car and getting out of Lisbon. I think I'll be stuck in that roundabout in my nightmares for quite a while."

"And you were just getting used to a standard again! But I'm glad you were the driver. I couldn't have handled that crazy roundabout. You were incredible—so calm."

"I don't know why, but it was like I was in some kind of bubble and could keep my head," she muses. "Things got much better, though, when we were out of the city."

"The drive north was beautiful, wasn't it? All those hills and olive groves. But then you had to navigate the tiny, twisty streets of Nazare."

"One moment I'll never forget was finally sitting down for dinner at the hotel at the end of that tough day, watching the sun set over the ocean and having our first sip of vinho verde." We share our first smile since this flight home began.

I sit back and let the camera rest in my lap. Marianne has become a very capable woman. She took charge of the car rental and got us to our hotel that first day; I'm not sure I could have done it. When we were children and adolescents, I was the one usually in control, but the power shifted as we grew older and she grew stronger. One thing I had wanted to find out on this trip was how we had emerged from our past and matured into the women we are now, what brokenness remains, and what healing has been done. I see more clearly than ever how strong Marianne is, how confidently she is able to deal with unfamiliar circumstances.

I pick up my camera again and click through the photos of our time in Nazare, deleting the duds as I go. There are some good ones, though, taken as we walked from our hotel down the steep, narrow, cobbled roads through the town to the beach. Our full day there was cool and cloudy, with the occasional light shower, yet the wide beach was still lined with the small tents—blue, white, striped—of vacationers. While I sat on the sand and wriggled my feet into its rough graininess, admiring its rose hue, Marianne ventured into the water. I watched her dip her toes in the ocean, take a few tentative steps in, and back out quickly at the shock of coldness. It was enough for me to watch the high, rolling waves, darker than the gray sky, stretch out to the endless, open horizon.

I show Marianne photos of us at the restaurant that evening, smiling and holding up our wine glasses as the ocean behind us gleamed in the setting sun. It had been a perfect day. After dinner, we had walked slowly back up through the town, strolling along the winding streets close with houses, in the deepening dusk. By the time we reached the top of the hill and left the town for the road to our hotel, it was dark. There were no streetlights to guide us, only the light of the stars and moon and the dark shapes of trees and bushes rising from the side of the road. I began to feel uneasy. Then, when the first car whizzed by us, too close for me, fear hit me like a wave, leaving me trembling.

"Mare," I had called to her, "walk at the side of the road. The cars go fast here, and they can't see us until they're almost on top of us."

"Don't worry, Lor," she called back, still walking in the middle of the road. "There are hardly any cars. And look at the sky!"

I glanced up and found she was right: the sky glittered with fields of stars, tiny ones and bright bold ones densely packed, more than I had ever seen before. But when another car came speeding up behind us a few minutes later, a second wave of fear overwhelmed me.

"Please, Mare," I begged her, "what you're doing is dangerous. I'm afraid something will happen to you." My voice was shaky and breathless.

She moved to the roadside reluctantly. I was ashamed that she was witnessing how fear could seize and incapacitate me. I knew I was overreacting, but I was in the grip of something I couldn't control, terrified of her coming to harm.

Marianne is looking at me now, grinning, and I shake myself loose from memory.

"We don't have any photos of the day we went north to the Douro. I'm really glad you were driving that day."

This surprises me. She's the bolder one; I'm the cautious hermit, afraid of using a GPS.

"Really? I thought you would have handled it better than I did," I tell her.

"No way, Lor! Creeping up the mountain on that tiny road with all those twists and turns? And a sheer drop beside us? In a standard?" Then she's laughing. "You were hysterical, though. Yelling and swearing at the top of your lungs." She imitates me in a way that draws stares from our fellow passengers. "'Why did we come on this fucking trip? Why did we choose this fucking place? I'm afraid of heights, for fuck's sake!' I hardly knew who was in the driver's seat."

"And you kept shouting at me: 'Keep going, Lor! Keep your eyes on the road! And don't look down!'" She's still laughing. "I'm sure I'll find the whole thing as funny as you do someday when I'm over the trauma."

"Thank goodness for that van, eh?" We pause to remember the kind young man who showed us how to get down to the river road. "Without him we might still be lost in the mountains somewhere."

"Hopefully, with a big jug of red wine, some olives, and a loaf of bread." I can smile now, a little. "Really, I think what saved us was that it never occurred to me we could meet a car coming the other way. I would have been completely paralyzed if I'd had that thought or if another car had actually come." I shudder briefly. "When we finally reached the river road, I was never so happy in my life to be on flat ground."

She smiles in my eyes and reaches over to squeeze my hand.

"But we made it, Lor, didn't we? What an adventure."

I smile back and we hold each other's gaze for a sweet moment, then sit back in amiable silence.

I wonder now if she was surprised during this trip to see how anxious and afraid I can be. The lingering legacy of trauma. She didn't call attention to my distress, though, just ignored it or took charge of things when necessary. And I won't mention to her how saddened I was to see the ways in which our past still shaped her.

She bonded with the three dogs that belonged to the owners of the quinta we stayed at in the Douro. They were big dogs of mixed breeds—one was a golden color and another seemed to have some German shepherd in it—all used to running free along the do Tedo River and the dirt lanes of the vineyards. They were clearly happy and well-cared for. Yet at the end of an elegant dinner Marianne and I shared one evening in Pinhao, she asked me for the remains of the lamb chops I had eaten. I was surprised but awkwardly scraped them onto her plate.

"What are you doing, Mare?" I asked as she withdrew a plastic bag from her pocket.

"I'm taking the scraps for the dogs."

"But why? They seem well-fed."

She just shrugged and shoved the food into the bag. When we arrived back at the quinta, she left the pile on a low stone fence where the dogs could easily find it. She must have sensed how strange I found this behavior because she said, quietly, before we turned into the corridor of our wing, "It's more for me than them."

I ponder this incident now. Marianne has always loved animals in a fierce way I can't fully understand, taking a beloved cat off to university with her, inviting strays into her home. She is protective of their innocence and vulnerability; maybe she can trust them with her own. But I didn't know until the evening in Pinhao how much she needs to rescue and care for them, even if they have no need of rescue. The little girl trying to make things better.

My way has been trying to fix things, big things and little things: placating our unstable mother to prevent a storm of rage; keeping an ordered home; addressing injustices I see at the university where I work. But mostly I've tried to fix myself, to give myself to the long healing process I've been in these past thirty years. I've recovered the memories, done the emotional work, and slowly, gradually become stronger, more peaceful. When I was a child, I tried at school to behave as the others did and perform well so people wouldn't see how hurt I was, how fragile. I wanted them to think I was normal and to accept me. Even now, I know how to conduct myself in the world so that people think I am strong and competent. But I still strive for internal wholeness, to be free of the fear and pain that linger and exhaust me sometimes, though few in my life know that now.

Marianne breaks into my ruminations with a nudge of her knee. "Hey, Lor. I think lunch is coming."

I poke my head up over the seats and see the attendant moving toward us with her cart. "Oh, good," I say, "I'm really hungry." The meals come—vegetarian pasta and chicken with rice; we order different ones so we can share.

"What were your favorite parts of the trip?" Marianne asks as we get through the limp vegetables that are supposed to be the salad.

"I liked our evenings at the quinta, lying on the bed reading and drinking wine together."

"It was nice just resting at the end of the day," she agrees. "I loved our full day in Nazare. Meandering from our hotel down through the town. Remember that little place we found for coffee halfway down? *Café com lette,* coffee with milk. Those were practically the only words we needed in Portuguese, and *obrigado,* thank you. When we finally got to the ocean, it was fun to be on the beach and shop at that market."

"A really sweet thing for me," I say, "was sharing a room in Nazare and then again in Lisbon. Do you realize we hadn't slept in the same room together since we were teenagers? It was so comforting to have you in the bed next to mine again. I slept well those nights."

"Me too." She is quiet for a moment. Then she spears some of my pasta and continues reminiscing. "Our last dinner in the Douro—in that little place in Folgorosa—was great. It was nice to be served by the daughter of the owner and kind of him to share some of his own port with us at the end of the evening."

"I liked being immersed in Portuguese life that night. But remember what you did after dinner? You bought some extra food and took it down to that man who was begging at the roadside. I really wondered what you were doing, approaching him alone and in the dark like that. You didn't know anything about him. I would have been too scared to do that."

"Oh, he seemed pretty harmless," she says. "Remember, Lor? We had seem him earlier in the day in Regua. He must have found a ride to Folgorosa to beg outside that fancy restaurant on the river, the one we couldn't afford. He was skinny and his jacket was too big for him, but he was polite, not pushy. He just seemed kind of sad to me."

Thinking about the man and Marianne's gesture, it strikes me that her kindness sometimes hits the mark, forges a real connection. I squirm a little inside at my own limitations.

We are interrupted as the attendant asks for our empty containers. Then Marianne smiles at me and pulls out her book again. "I'm at an exciting part, when Ian and Sarah reunite. I want to get through it before the flight is over."

"No problem," I reply. I need some time to myself, anyway. I can't shake from my mind the sight of Marianne handing over money and food to the thin, middle-aged stranger in the ill-fitting suit. He looked so grateful. I watched from a short distance as they chatted together for a few minutes. Then he shook her hand and moved away.

I know I love well the people in my life. But they're safe. I'm anxious around the ones on the periphery: the drunks warming themselves in the foyer of the bank where the instant tellers are;

the career beggar with her walker and missing teeth calling to me on the street. I'm afraid they'll try to take from me something I don't have to give. I shift in my seat, trying to stretch my legs a bit. I wish I could settle into a book like Marianne, but I'm too fidgety. Something is poking at my consciousness. I get up, ease my way around her, and walk up and down the aisles for a while, still thinking, pondering the kind of love I witnessed Marianne extending. Finally, after returning to my seat, I reach for the airline magazine and flip through the pages, hoping for an article that will capture and keep my attention. But the photos—of vivid turquoise seas, white beaches, and women in colorful clothing—assault my senses. I return the magazine to its pocket and rest my head back in my seat. Maybe I'll try to sleep a little. I close my eyes and attempt to slow my breathing, empty my mind. But it's no use. My thoughts insist on taking me back to the scene with the man and Marianne, and this time a door opens in my consciousness. I imagine myself in the man's place, cold and alone in the dark outside the restaurant. Marianne is reaching toward me and I take her gift of food, listening to the warmth in her voice, though I can't fully understand her words. A slight tremor moves beneath my ribcage. I wonder at it, then am startled by the captain's voice once again filling the cabin.

"Ladies and gentleman, we are now beginning our descent to Toronto and will be arriving at Pearson International Airport in about fifteen minutes, 3:21 local time." The pressure beneath my ribcage continues. Then the light above our seats comes on and I move to fasten my seatbelt. Marianne leans forward to put her book away, and we shove our bags under the seats in front of us.

"Look, Mare, can you see?" I try to speak normally and point to the window. "We're over Lake Ontario now, and the shoreline is just ahead. We're almost home."

"It was a great trip, but it'll be good to be back," she says, stretching her arms over her head.

"Mare, I—," I turn to her, but I don't know what to say.

"Are you okay, Lor?" She must see the distress in my eyes. "What's wrong?"

"I can't stop thinking about you and the poor man you helped." I'm finding it hard to breathe and not because we're losing altitude. I feel like I'm on the verge of learning something, something big. I'm reaching toward it, or rather it is reaching toward me.

"You love people and animals as they are—destitute, sick,

homeless." How can I say what I'm seeing for the first time? "I've tried so hard to get better all these years, to heal from the past, to become whole—you know me." She nods. "But, maybe . . ." I look full into her eyes, eyes shining green in the light from the window. The plane drops lower.

"Maybe it's better to be loved, maybe I can be loved, as you love the weak ones. Maybe I can be loved just as I am, still broken in some ways. Maybe I don't have to try so hard to be well anymore . . ." The plane is dropping quickly, now, the earth rushing up to meet us. I grasp the handrests as I sense myself losing my grip on my safe, ordered life. I can't find my breath. I feel Marianne's hand on my mine, let her pull it into hers.

"It's okay, Lor. I've got you." The plane bumps onto the runway. "Everything is all right. Everything'll be all right. We're home."

# PART NINE

# Emergence Continues

S OMETIMES TROUBLE COMES HURTLING OUT OF THE darkness and knocks you flat before you can see it and brace yourself. In May 2015, I was bent over my work at my program coordinator's desk at the Writing Center when my manager poked her head into my office and asked me to follow her. She led me into another office where two women were seated at a round table: my union president and a representative from human resources. One of the women began reading to me from an official document while my manager stood silently by, her face pale and strained. Fragments of meaning began to enter my already numbed mind: my position had been made redundant. After a few moments, I lifted my hand and interrupted the speaker. "I know you're talking to me," I managed, "but I have no idea what you're saying." The other woman, kinder, explained the situation more slowly. Then she offered to get my things from my office before walking me out of the building.

I sat on a stone bench, now alone, stunned. Then I did three wise things: I gave myself some time to sit and absorb what had just happened; I listened to flecks of birdsong from the line of young oaks along the sidewalk, watched sunlight glinting from passing cars, and registered the new bleakness in my belly; then I prayed. I asked God to increase my capacity for trust and to guide me forward. Finally, I stood and walked directly to the campus building that housed the distance studies program. I found the director, told her about my situation, and asked if my teaching load there might be secured and possibly increased. Over the next weeks, I shored up my remaining work at the university and began to look for other teaching opportunities.

Two months later, trouble struck again. The drought of framing orders and art sales in Ray's business accompanying the intense heat of that summer brought him to financial crisis. Only my severance pay enabled his business to continue. His confidence in his livelihood shaken, Ray stumbled into despair.

At the end of September, we were hit with a final blow that came, as terrible news often does, by way of a phone call. My sister's voice, trembling, telling me that her best friend, our lifetime surrogate sister, had suffered a sudden heart attack and lay in a coma in a hospital. I made the trip back to my hometown in time to say goodbye. I entered Cindy's room, brushed her fine auburn hair from her forehead, and thanked her for being home for me in a way few others ever had. The next day, I again stood at her bedside, this time as part of a circle of close loved ones, as she was removed from life support, and her gentle light left the world.

The darkness I entered that fall was thick and black. The blows I had sustained had opened the deep sense of disaster that my childhood experiences had left in me. Overwhelmed by the dread, pain, and hopelessness of it, all I could do was search for ways to continue living, hour by hour. The worst of my thoughts and feelings told me God had abandoned me in both my past and my present. I was utterly forsaken.

But as the fall days gave way to the grayness of November, the intensity of the darkness eased, just a little. The desperate question that had always burned at the core of my being—where was God in my suffering, when my life shattered as a child, when disaster had recently struck?—began to seem less urgent. At last I let the question go, let myself settle into mystery; for the first time in my life, it was all right not to know. The darkness began to have something of peace in it.

Soon after, I was sitting in the waiting room of a local garage surrounded by the muffled sounds of men's voices and the wheezing of lifts and spray guns. My car was being rust-proofed, and I had decided to stay until it was done. I began writing in my journal, looking up from time to time at the brown vinyl chairs in the otherwise empty room or out the window at the bare black branches of trees. My solitude and this time apart helped me to write about the despair that was now slowly dissipating. Then, as I wrote, the answer came, the answer to the question I had let go of. Now I knew where God was when my parents betrayed and hurt me. I heard in my spirit a single word: brooding. God was brooding over me.

In the months that followed, I pondered the brooding God that in the creation story hovered over the face of the deep. The brooding love that, like a mother hen, gathers her chicks under her wings. I came to understand myself as dwelling under those wings: "You who live in the shelter of the Most High, who abide in the shadow of the Almighty, will say to the Lord, 'My refuge and my fortress; my God, in whom I trust.'" (Psalm 91:1–2, NRSV). That sense of being closely attended to, protected, and comforted began to seep into my psyche.

As I continued my teaching work at the university, now with a lighter load, and moved more deeply into community life at church, internal shifts kept happening. In the spring of 2017, I felt compelled to share with my pastors the important details of my childhood and healing journey. I was certain that when I told them my story a stone would roll away from the tomb of my past, and I would be free to emerge. The telling ushered in a stage of my life marked by Lazarus experiences as I was called forth into community and greater visibility, into using my voice in a new way.

One evening a friend and I went to a poetry reading at a retreat center deep in the woods. I had long admired the poet for the bracing clarity of both her verse and memoir writing. When I spoke with her after the reading, I told her of my reluctance to write openly about what had happened to me as a child for fear of overwhelming a reader.

"Don't write for the reader," she ordered in her forthright way. "Just write. And don't underestimate the reader, who is likely wiser and tougher than you think." I thought about this for a moment.

"So I should just go for broke," I ventured.

"Just go for broke," she said. "Promise me you'll go for broke."

Speaking the truth of my past to my faith community and hearing this poet's admonition gave me a new freedom to bring my story from the shadows and into the now open horizon before me.

# Emergence

My eyes, bound shut. Air in my nostrils, foul.
I seem to be in a cloud of stench. Try sound.
I will my lips apart, push up through my throat:
a croaking whisper. My arms, my legs, where?—
one with the blackness, the hard ground more real
than my body. My mind a small island of sense.

Behind me a floating warmth, murmuring. Voices?
Where am I? Flashes, images—Martha's face,
worn and worried, near mine. My own frail hand
on a rough blanket. A feeling of water, cold,
trickling from the sides of my mouth, unswallowed.
An overtaking darkness. I am in the grave.

Claimed. I know it now, death, have felt it
moving through my veins. Delivering me
to my memories. Of being a boy snatched
and dragged into a shadowed alley, shoved
to a wall by strong hands. Searing pain. Of home
and harsh voices tearing the air, shards of sound.
Absences. My crippled passage into manhood.
Later, learning to shirk, to hide my shame.
Shirking even Him, hiding even from Him.

Death has delivered me to fear, my constricted heart
a fist in my chest thumping hard, fast. No one
must see the seeping wound that has driven me
to skulking in the night, robbing others of that
which was wrenched from me. Hating Mary's singing,
Martha's able hands. Death gives me to myself
in the covering of night, a merciful reckoning.
A shadow passing not by, but through, in ragged
remembering, unmembering. Old life decomposed.

The warmth behind moves into me, sets off
a spreading tingling, tiny needles sharp beneath
my skin. Then strength pushes in, calms the prickling,
brings the need to move. A first shuffle of limbs
and rags across the earth, a small lift of my hand.
Murmuring resolves into words, a voice. My name

and a command to leave. Lazarus, come forth.
Arms and legs pulled to crawling by a silver string
of sound. They move toward the voice, then falter.
Who calls me? To what?—the chattering, the jostling,
the stares. I a freak in tatters, clawing from the tomb,
blinded by grave clothes, then by light. No more

master of shadows and hiding places. Should I stay
safe in the darkness—quiet, alone—but make Him
a fraud? I know now it is He who calls. I know Him.
He will not show the world the wretch I was. He saw
my skulking ways, let me seek and find this tomb.
Will let me stay here, will roll the stone in place Himself.

This knowing brings me joy. Yet is there more?
Does He see something else in me, that He should call
me forth? Maybe He knows how much I love Him,
and my sisters. That I want light more than shadows.
Can I stand? Lurching to my feet, I totter forward.
The noise ahead is now a roaring. Martha. Mary.

Maybe I can live there, now, in that light. I push
my right leg forward, then my left. Strength grows,
more steps. More warmth. Inside the sagging cloth,
I feel clean. New. I reach my hands before me,
feeling my way. He is waiting, waiting for me. For us.

# My Emerging Self

Emerging from the tomb of my past, from decades of memory work, I moved into changes in most spheres of my life. At the university, I received a promotion to assistant professor. Although I continued to meet with students on campus at the Writing Center, my chief position was now as an online writing teacher, so I spent most of my time in my study at home. My work life was more stable and supported than it had ever been, awash in grace. I could sit at my desk marking assignments with my favorite music quietly playing in the background. Lift my head from time to time to the sight of my garden in bloom or blanketed with snow. "For my yoke is easy, and my burden is light," (Matt. 11:30, ESV) Jesus said, and the beautiful weight of that load sat perfectly on my shoulders.

My writing life also became truer to my emerging self. After publishing some early short stories and poems, I had bogged down under the pile of rejections that increasingly robbed me of my confidence. Finally, one afternoon while sitting on a rock in a river near my writing studio, I howled out my discouragement to God and gave up. I would stop sending out my work for the present and indeterminate future. I had ceased to write for the reader; now I would no longer write for the publisher. I became free to listen without distraction to the Spirit speaking within me and to write what I heard as truthfully as I could.

Arriving more fully in the present also meant being divested of my grave clothes, the emotional vestiges of my past. One by one over the next couple of years, I lost the ways I had developed from early childhood to survive the trauma of life in my home. The mental blindness that had kept me from full consciousness of my situation dissolved, and I was flooded with a new and terrible awareness. My pattern of trying to ensure my safety by fusing, first with my mother and then with any other potentially threatening authority figure, left me. Without the illusion of control my people-pleasing ways had given me, I felt exposed and vulnerable, for a time very fragile. Finally, I was freed of my striving—of my urgent compulsion to keep moving forward at all costs, my drive to do something, anything, to make life better. As I lost these grave clothes, the feelings that my coping ways had kept at bay rose up and through me.

*A new day's joy comes slowly.*
*Mourning dogs a beginning,*
*nips the heels of just opened.*
*Did Lazarus, stumbling*
*startled into light, new life lived*
*in wonder of the ordinary,*
*feel echoes of the grave?*
*An honoring of sorrow.*
*Ointment-soaked strips of remembering*
*the long struggle in the night.*

These years of healing were painful, sometimes fear-filled, and often exhausting, but tremendous gifts came to me during this time. I began to feel the pleasure of personhood, the value of a self I was now able to protect. On Sunday afternoons, I could stand on a mat in the middle of our living room, stretch, and breathe into a body that felt increasingly like my own. I would start with mountain pose, pressing my heels into the ground and lifting the crown of my head, enjoying the strength and freedom of my elongated spine. Then I would set my shoulders back, open my arms, and raise my chest, feeling my ribs expand as I filled with breath—breath that brought new courage to a part of myself that had caved in, shrinking from life. Later, in child pose, lying face down with my arms stretched out in front of me and my knees splayed out to the sides, I breathed to open my hips and the back of my pelvis, inviting Holy Spirit healing into this most broken of places. A body opening, strengthening, becoming free and clean.

And the little one inside of me, who had been nurtured well for so long, began awakening into joy. One sunny summer morning after a meeting on campus, I ducked into a washroom in the library. The building was quiet, so I lingered in front of the washroom mirror, examining a front tooth that had recently been repaired. Suddenly I was suffused, from head to toe, with gratefulness. Mimicking a little girl I had seen in a YouTube video, I looked myself in the eye and said out loud, "I love my tooth." Pause. "I love my tooth. I love my shirt." My voice started to grow louder. "I love my job, I love my students." I was picking up steam. "I love my city. I love my home." I thrust my arms into the air, triumphant. "I love my friends!" I was stomping now. "I LOVE MY SISTER! I...LOVE...RAY!!" As I was at full tilt, the door opened. I quickly lowered my arms. I didn't dare glance at the woman who had entered the washroom, but I did give myself a sly smile in the mirror on my way out.

I also started to experience the world as a more positive, supportive place than I had ever understood it to be. Just after I received my promotion, I was stopped in the hall of a campus building by a woman who had been on the committee considering my application.

"It was an easy decision," she confided. "When your application came up, there was a lot of enthusiasm around the table. Congratulations! Well deserved." Her words, her smile, the touch of her hand on my shoulder sent the strength of that support straight into my bones. I left the building in wonder as my mind slowly caught up. Maybe I could stop bracing for disaster and instead trust in others' regard for me and in God's abiding love. During these years, as Lazarus did, I came forth into community, surrounded by colleagues and friends and a church family witnessing my transformation and loving me through it. I was finding home in the world.

# PART TEN

# Place: The Present

O NE EVENING RECENTLY, I WAS CURLED UP AT THE
end of a big leather couch in the basement of my friend
Claire. We had begun as colleagues at The Writing
Center but quickly became friends as we discovered a shared
love of certain authors, of gardening, of making good homes for
ourselves and our loved ones. But more—we shared a certain
sensibility, sensitivity really, to the presence and movement of
God's Spirit. We enjoyed talking together about both the details
of our lives and the mysteries of faith. This particular evening,
we were sipping wine and catching up on each other's lives, and
I was telling her about the healing that was happening in mine.
We began to talk about faith, and suddenly she quoted, in her
clear, silvery voice: "All shall be well, and all shall be well; all
manner of thing shall be well," from the writings of medieval
mystic Julian of Norwich. I was astonished to hear these words
in this context, but they transported us both to a place where we
could believe that, at the foundation, everything was all right.

A few days later at home, as I was engrossed in the memoir I
was reading, the words of Julian came to me again, this time silently
from the page before me: "All shall be well, and all shall be well;
all manner of thing shall be well." I held my breath at the wonder
of it, then breathed the words deep into my body and spirit. The
following Sunday at church, I was approached after the service by
a great, kind bear of a man who offered to pray for me. His hand
was heavy on my shoulder as he asked God to give me the strength
I needed. Then the tenor of his prayer changed to reassurance.

"Things will get better," he said. "All shall be well. All shall be well." An anchor in my solidifying life in the world around me.

# City Park in Autumn

Some, fully dressed, chatter together
as their leaves lift and rustle in the wind.
Some, flaunting, flick to show both sides
of their leaves, vivid green as in spring.

Some, half-denuded, murmur in small
distressed whispers to those shamed like them,
hoping that no one will see another dry,
curling leaf desert another quivering limb.

Some stand silent—raising bare branches
in admonition of those still bold
in their fluttering gold and scarlet—
disdainful of the nattering, frivolous ones.

But some, oh some (and let me be one of these),
say nothing, see nothing but the sky
they reach for in simple, naked praise.

# Snow

Another heavy fall in Kingston. Late February—
winter should be easing its grip, gray snowbanks
sinking. But underfoot the hard-packed whiteness
creaks, and my scarf begins to sag, breath-soaked.

I seek diagonals as I walk—the shortest
route from one place to another. My footsteps
groove those slanted places deep. At the churchyard,
though, a drift blocks the way. I stop, consider,
turn back to follow the cleared sidewalk
to the corner, pedestrian on a slow path.

Across the street, the tattoo parlor's neon sign
glows in the shadow of dusk. Cars at the stoplight
sigh gray curls. Kitty-corner, red brick shops sit
beneath a slope of snow. In the world still hunkered
under winter's weight, breaths are puffs of vapor rising,
all time is waiting. Waiting and watching. Listening.

The snow teaches me, the gift of snow too deep
for passing. Someday I might choose the slower way,
might not need the blocked path. If I can't, then,
thank God, the snow will come again.

# Touchstones

I'm heading to the laundromat today. I live in a mixed neighborhood of student renters and homeowners in the downtown core of this small, historic university town, so the laundromat is convenient, just two blocks away. Still, I take my car; I have mountains of clothes to haul there and back. I gather soap and change, sort the clothes into whites and darks, and heave the baskets into the car.

I have been going to this laundromat for thirty years, all my married life. I know that new acquaintances think this habit is odd. Ray and I could put a washer and dryer in our basement. But although we love this old red brick house that has been such a great gift to us, the cellar is dark, low-ceilinged and sometimes damp, not a place I enjoy. I like the bright spaciousness of the laundromat, and I like the efficiency of using the big machines to wash and dry a lot of laundry at once. Still, it is a big job. In our first decade of marriage, when I lived quietly and gently through intense years of healing from my childhood, the chore often seemed too much for me, so I always prayed for a special provision of grace. I needed God in the details of finding a parking spot and gaining access to both the big machines and a full table for folding. Now I am much stronger, but I'm still grateful to feel myself carried through laundry day.

After I pull the car up to the squat, low-slung building, I prop a basket on my hip, struggle through the March slush, and swing myself through the front door. The place is quiet this morning, as I'd hoped. I pack my clothes into two triple-loaders and get additional change from Mike at the front desk. The familiar swish of water begins in the washers as I settle in a chair with my book. Morning light is falling through the window at my back onto the long table in front of me. Though no one else is in my alley, the head and shoulders of a young man poke up from behind the machines in the next one. He has a dark beard and glasses, buds in his ears, and a leather university jacket. A woman with frazzled brassy hair trudges by; she has piles of laundry as large as mine and searches out the other triple-loaders. Soon a burst of chatter at the front door signals the entrance of two young women, more students. I'm glad when they pass my alley and move on.

There are the regulars, like me, and the occasional customers. It's easy to tell the occasionals: whether they're tourists from the nearby marina or homeowners spring washing their large bedding, they all look a bit disoriented and need advice about how to use the machines. I love the mix of regulars—students, of course, and other renters who are sometimes under-employed—but the ones who sadden me are the old men, who often seem lonely and somewhat lost. Being surrounded by people outside my normal circle of friends and colleagues, everyone engaged in the intimate task of washing clothes, comforts and connects me, affirms that we are all in this undertaking of life together.

I also appreciate the owners who have been here through the years. Mike is the youngest one I've known, his pleasant scruffiness at odds with a reserve that could be shyness. Mike of the smoke breaks and the world inside his laptop. Vera works here for Mike as an attendant; I see her less often because she works the afternoon shift, but I enjoy her industrious management of the place. Her soft curling white hair suggests she is in her seventies, but she wears slim jeans and moves in the energetic way of someone much younger. Today I inquire of Mike about Tony, who owned the place before Mike and worked here in his later years because I'm sure he couldn't stand to be idle. I usually tried to limit my chats with Tony because of his unrelenting pessimism, but we respected each other, and I loved his gallant insistence on carrying one of my full laundry baskets back to my car. Even in the last year, as he grew noticeably thin and began wearing a toque, and I knew my strength exceeded his, he did not allow me to carry my loads alone. Mike tells me now that Tony died of cancer two weeks ago.

I absorb this loss as I pull warm clothes from the dryers, heap shirts and pajamas and socks on a table, and move into the rhythm of folding. I bring a sweater to my face and breathe in its fresh scent. Then I place it on its front before me, tuck its sleeves behind, and fold it in half to make a square before starting a pile in the basket. As I work the fabric of each article through my hands, feeling and shaping it, I am carried by touch and motion into a flow, like prayer. The hum of the washing machines and the steady soft thumping of clothes in the dryers accompany me in this hymn to the ordinary. To this loose, fluid community brought together only by the shared necessities of the body. Later, as I call out a farewell to Mike, carrying my second basket to my car myself, I feel Tony hovering and helping in whatever way his spirit now can.

After returning home, putting away the laundry, and having lunch, I set out on foot to a meeting at the university campus. To get there, I walk several blocks to the city's main street, Princess Street, beautiful with its red brick and limestone shops and restaurants stretching all the way down to the lake. I still pause to admire storefronts, their intricate brickwork framing tall windows, their old limestone blocks weathered but solid in walls that have stood for centuries.

The bell tinkles as I enter my husband's art gallery and framing shop. I usually stop in for coffee and a quick chat on my way to campus. The space is tall and narrow; filled salon-style with paintings in oil, acrylic, and encaustic, it is a former carriageway that once served as a passage between taverns and shops on the street and the stone horses' stable to the rear. Ray enjoys telling visitors of the likelihood that Sir John A. Macdonald, our country's first prime minister, often passed through to stable his horse before settling in at the Royal Tap Room, a favorite public house of his that still exists today.

"Hi, Lovey," I call. "It's just me."

Soon he emerges from the gallery's back room, smiling, already with a mug in hand for me. I move toward the desk where he helps his customers choose frames; he joins me there and slides the mug over. We share details of the day before I give him a quick hug and leave through the back way. I pause after I shut the door and feel the sun's new warmth. It was a mild, slushy day like this more than three decades ago when I made my way to this door, seeking the comfort of his friendship. Over many years since then, I have watched as customers and friends have come to and through this shop, have experienced Ray's nurturing, wise presence in what I now see as this passageway of grace.

After I leave, I walk through a student neighborhood where the houses eventually give way to the limestone buildings of the university. The campus is compact, with buildings clustered on several large city blocks rising from the lakefront. Today the halls of stone and glass, old and new, stand bare without their covering of spring green or crimson autumn ivy. I choose a route behind the old library, then stop and lay a gloved hand on the stone railing of steps leading up to heavy oak doors. I breathe in what I know to be the rarefied air surrounding these halls and marvel at my place within them.

I first experienced this university in November of my final year in high school. A few classmates with whom I was touring postsecondary schools wanted to explore the campus, so I came along, though I knew I would never attend. The city was too far from my hometown, and no one I knew well would be coming here. Still, the evening after our arrival I found myself standing alone in the middle of an almost deserted campus. I paused for a while to admire the old buildings surrounding me: the red brick of the university art gallery, the graceful stone arches and curving staircases of a building across the street. Beside it, the clock tower of an older limestone building was fading into the purple dusk. Snow fell gently and quietly around me. Then, in the strange and wonderful hush of the moment, I was struck suddenly with conviction. I knew with absolute certainty that this was the place for me.

And it was a good place to be. I became involved in a community of faith that sheltered and supported me. I was stimulated by my studies in literature and politics, though I wasn't able to achieve as well as I would have liked. Then, after my time as a student, I lost confidence in my value to the world. All my strength went inward for so long that when it came time for me to re-enter the workplace, I was sure I'd have to take a job at a fast-food or retail business. I couldn't imagine working at the university where I had struggled so hard as a student.

Now I emerge from behind the library onto one of the wide avenues bisecting the campus. My paths from building to building are familiar, and I now walk them with confidence. I cross the street and climb the steps to Dunning Hall, lately renovated to house the offices of the faculty of arts and science. I am here to meet with a team of colleagues to discuss the development of a new writing course. After the meeting, I decide to take a way I rarely walk and head down University Avenue toward the lake. At the bottom of the street, I pause to consider a little yellow house and remember. The house still seems oddly placed here, with its dormers and wide green-shuttered windows, between the square, modern building of the campus's health services and the towering old limestone hospital on the other side. This house used to be the university's Writing Center, the site of my first job after my student and intensive healing years. The house looks worn now and its lawn today is sodden and brown, the air full of the damp of early spring.

It was a September day when I left the hermitage of my home to walk, trembling in my shoes, the long stone path from the street to this house's front door. That day I was unaware of the golden light or the leaves turning on the cherry trees bordering the yard. I shook inwardly because I still felt like a black sheep on campus, like I didn't belong here. I was inexperienced in the working world and hadn't been a student for twelve years, much less tutored one. Still, the director of the center took a chance and assigned me to several four-hour shifts per week. A gracious, quiet-spoken man, Doug brought his beagle to the house every day and had a gift for creating a warm, supportive community of teachers and writers, many of whom would become friends. He provided me with the most gentle of passages into my working life.

As I walked the stone path that first September day, I asked God to bless me in this place, to go before and beside me. God hovered during my days of sitting at a desk beside a student, both of us bent over words that attempted, fumblingly or elegantly, to express thoughts sometimes only newly forming. I would listen to a second-year student read to me her ideas about the spiritual significance of gothic architecture, the lake visible and sparkling through the window and the dog snoring in a sunbeam near our feet. I smile as I remember one sweet, funny student, so taken with the coziness of our little house that she blurted out, "Do you all live here?" As I pause here in front of the center, I think of days that turned to years of fulfilling work tutoring, then teaching courses, and then supporting and mentoring other tutors and teachers.

Setbacks and disappointments in my career have come, as they do so often in institutional life. Losing a job and experiencing conflicts with colleagues have shown me at times how much I have to learn or how unkind large organizations can be. These challenges have also touched my deep inner sense of insecurity and my long-steeped distrust of the world. They have rocked my feeling of being safe in it.

I turn from the house and resume my walk. A familiar mix of emotions blows through me as the quickening wind blows through my hair. The surge of gratitude for the privilege of working with students who inspire me with their eagerness and energy, their hopefulness. The sense of my lingering fragility in balance with my growing strength and ability. The deep-down feeling that my place in the world must always be grounded in the One who made me and set me here.

I remember that it is Thursday, a market day. Though few vendors usually appear when it is this cold, Steve will be there with his cider and apples and maybe some potted spring flowers. I'll do a few errands before I head home for the day. I reach the edge of campus and cross the street to City Park, a huge expanse that includes playing fields, rolling lawns, and towering trees, both deciduous and coniferous. As I enter the park, I glance to my left past the baseball diamond to where the old limestone courthouse sits on a rise at the edge of the park, its four huge pillars solid beneath its central dome. In the distance on my right, the lake shifts and glints behind the grand houses of King Street. As I step around melting ice patches on the path that runs diagonally through the park, the trees' early spring bareness allows a stronger sense than usual of this town's past. As the first capital of Canada, the city enjoyed an early though brief burst of trade and institutional life that gave rise to the noble buildings—the university halls, the courthouse, the mansions of wealthy merchants—that still surround this park. I stop and stretch my arms to the sky, the yellowed grass spreading around me, the lake stretching to an imperceptible horizon, all this openness cradled in the solidness of brick and stone.

Leaving the park, I walk several blocks along King Street toward the market square. As commercial buildings begin to replace the large old residential homes, the hum of traffic invades my consciousness. The market comes into view ahead. Though the square nestles behind the majestic limestone city hall, it still seems to catch and hold the swirling winds that blow in off the lake. As I expected, Steve is one of only a few vendors today. His collar is turned up against the chill but he seems otherwise unperturbed. His sturdy body is built to withstand any weather, and his face wears the ruddiness of a man who spends days and months outside.

"Hey, Steve," I greet him. "Pretty windy today, eh?"

"Ah, it's not bad," he replies, uncharacteristically cheerful.

I pay for my cider and then decide to add a pot of budding daffodils, but this means I don't leave quickly enough to avoid Steve's inevitable complaints. Today they are about his current helper, who must be somewhere on a break. I decide to cut off the stream of discontent and admire his display of flowers before saying goodbye. Despite his gruffness, I'm fond of him. I've been coming to his stand on this corner for many years. I know that the quality of the fruit, vegetables, and plants he sells matters to him, and his good heart is stronger than his bluster.

I walk the next block to the main street and duck in at the health food store. The wide red brick building, with its gold- and green-painted trim, is always inviting, but particularly on this stubbornly chilly day. I step into warmth: besides the heat of the store there is the earthy smell of grains and spices, the sight of barley and rice in their bins and loaves of bread lined up on wooden shelves. Old oak floors creak underfoot. At the spice bins, I fill little bags with cinnamon, peppercorns, paprika, and dried thyme. I move deeper into the store for almonds, then drop several boxes of herbal teas into my basket. Sarah is at the cash register today, smiling at me in her quiet, serious way behind wire-rimmed glasses. When I held a yard sale at my house last fall, we discovered we were neighbors; now she always greets me by name. Today we chat about the slow coming of spring and our eagerness for a glimpse of green shoots in our gardens.

Out on the street again, the sidewalk is busy with young people in tight groups and older folks strolling slowly along. I pass the bakery—not today—and continue for several blocks to the coffee shop on the corner of my street. I'll get a latte to take home. Inside, the shop is filled with students peering intently at their laptop screens. I make my way to the counter as the fragrance of coffee and baked goods embraces me. Then I shift my load of purchases to free a hand for my latte and leave the shop.

The sidewalks are quieter off the main street. At the intersection before my block, I turn my head to excited barking up the street. Two dogs, not quite restrained by their owners, are rearing and pawing at each other in front of the laundromat. A woman with a full basket of clothes is trying to make her way around them. I smile at the scene and then set my sights for home. Past the public school, I reach my house, glad to be returning to it. The streets and buildings I inhabit enclose my life; the people I encounter fill it with color and warmth. Together they restore me—repair the broken places with the stones of security, the bricks of stability, the mortar of kindness and connection. They hold me as I slowly come to find myself safe and loved in the hand of God.

# Invitation

Come, Lord Jesus. Come
into our barren places. The wasted field,
the empty chair, the phone that will not ring,
the loss, the lack, the well of loneliness
that will not fill. Come.

Come, Lord Jesus. Come
into our busy places. The harried mind,
the hurried step, the hands that grip the wheel,
the needs, the tasks, the unrelenting drive
that will not stop. Come.

Come, Lord Jesus. Come
into our broken places. The crippled back,
the shattered life, the head bent low in shame,
the guilt, the rage, the bitter lance of grief
that will not leave. Come.

Come as You came in flesh
to empty stable, to noise and fray, to broken world.
Come fill, still, mend us.

Now as you come in spirit, you call:
Come, child. I will fill your thirsty soul
with my goodness that restores.
Come, child. I will still your troubled mind
in the shelter of my peace.
Come, child. I will mend your hurting heart
with my love that never fails.
Come, my child. Come.

# Epilogue

THIS SUMMER IS A QUIET ONE. I HAVE ONLY A SMALL group of students in my writing course and no consulting work on campus. Ray and I have no plans for major trips; we are staying close to home. Visitors will come, but only those close to us, and one at a time.

I'm grateful for the slower, easier pace, one that allows what I think is a major inner transformation to occur. Recently, I found that my feelings weren't working as they used to or sometimes seemed to be not working at all. Instead of experiencing my usual pleasure in spending time with friends or engaging in favorite activities, I felt nothing—not depressed, just a strange kind of blankness. At the same time, and thankfully, I also found myself no longer able to slide down negative rabbit holes in my feelings: to perceive a friend's emotional distance as a reason for insecurity or to become discouraged by less than ideal circumstances. My inner life appeared to be in flux.

The only insight I've been given is that I seem to be in the middle of a foundational shift, from trauma to rest. So much of my identity has been formed around surviving my childhood, learning to cope and find my way in the world despite my damaged psyche, and then devoting myself to long decades of healing. Now I find myself being reoriented: from living according to my old ways of understanding myself and being in the world to coming to rest in the arms of God. To arriving or returning to that warm, protected place that a child knows in the cradle of a parent's body, where everything is all right.

I have been deeply tired and easily overwhelmed, and that is because, I think, the transition is so profound. It is a homecoming.

166

Sinking into a new, peaceful state of being is not something I am accomplishing myself; the miracle is far beyond anything I could do to help it along. This is God's work. "Be held and behold," I heard in my spirit a few months ago, and those seem to be the words for this time. Be held and behold.

The foundational shift I am experiencing for a while had me feeling disconnected, like floating between one place and another. It seems I needed to move internally from my life oriented in trauma through a state of feeling unattached before beginning to connect. Now I am learning about connection.

I recently read a helpful chapter in a wonderful book, *Braiding Sweetgrass*, about lichens. A lichen is a gray/green spongy, disk-like plant that is a combination fungus and alga, often found on a rock face. It is the most ancient form of life. While its edges can be loose and ruffled, at its center it has a small, puckered circle, like a navel. This core of a lichen is where it attaches, with its acid carrying filaments, to a smooth, hard wall of rock.

I am a lichen, attaching to the rock that is God. This is an unexpected aspect of coming into a state of rest: being connected to a new, solid, safe, loving center, to God as my Mother and Father. As this connection takes place, I feel it physically in my core, right in my solar plexus. The rest of my body is slowly relaxing, giving up the aches of hypervigilance and self-protection. My emotions have returned; they are changeable these days and sometimes intense. I may feel angry for seemingly no reason, and often I find myself lifting my arms for joy. A transformation of my vision means that I'm starting to see the woman I've become, and I can look at the world as a beautiful, supportive, Spirit-infused place, despite its sometimes terrible realities. As I am being, as the apostle Paul says, "rooted and grounded in love," (Eph. 3:17, ESV) I am opening, awakening, and coming alive in a new way.

Now I try to live most days listening. Especially if I have unstructured time with no meetings or consulting shifts on campus, I try to discern and follow the gentle leading of the Spirit, to live each moment connected. I may take an early morning walk along the river, stopping sometimes to watch the water rippling in the sunlight. Or I may settle into a late breakfast at the computer, checking emails, after Ray has left for work. Midmorning I rise from my desk and pad into the kitchen to make a latte. While the machine hisses and gurgles, I choose some music, maybe something happy. Then, again at my desk with latte in hand and the rhythms of African music quietly dancing in the background, I turn my attention to a substantial piece of work, maybe some essays to mark or preparations to make for the upcoming term.

Later in the afternoon, it's time to shift from desk work to doing errands downtown. I think about the guests coming for the weekend and the meals I'll need to provide and plan the route of shops to visit. Stress starts tingling at the edge of my consciousness, and my shoulders begin to tighten. I slow myself down a bit and breathe. A soft nudge alters my thinking, and suddenly I see a better way. I can put a few things off until tomorrow and enlist Ray's help to lighten the load. I sling my errand-bag over my shoulder and leave the house, pausing to note the brown-eyed Susans blooming in the garden. As I start toward Princess Street, the motion of walking stretches and swings my body open, loosening my hips and reminding me to ease my shoulders back. A surge of joy comes as I round the corner and join the others on the crowded sidewalk. I weave my way through the slower pedestrians, feeling my body's strength as I move in the flow of life around me. I am fully myself and fully immersed in the One in whom I live and move and have my being.

Yesterday I began the drive home from my writing studio. I always feel a lovely sense of calm and gratitude as I wind my way through the trees along the gravel road, like my life is soaked with goodness. I turned onto the rural highway toward the city and switched on some music. A woman's silvery voice filled the car. The words of a favorite song flowed around me; then a stream moved straight into my heart:

*Through it all, through it all*
*my eyes are on You.*
*Through it all, through it all*
*it is well.*

I turned up the volume and began to sing along:

*Through it all, through it all*
*my eyes are on You,*
*and it is well with me.*

The road descended through a cutting and limestone walls rose up beside me as my voice rose to its full strength:

So let go my soul and trust in Him;
the waves and wind still know His name.

As I descended through the cutting, my city spread out before me, the lake glittering to the left, the domes and spires of buildings in the near distance, the road to home straight ahead. Suddenly, I was singing to my father, my mother. To my mother and father as tears streamed down my face:

It is well with my soul.
It is well, it is well with my soul.

It is well with me.

# Endnotes

1. "My Father's World" was written by Maltbie Davenport Babcock (1858–1901), an American clergyman and writer. After his death, his wife compiled and published a collection of his writings, which included this poem. The poem was set to music in 1915 by Franklin L. Sheppard, a friend of Babcock.

2. "Fairest Lord Jesus" was written in the seventeenth century in Germany. It was set to music by Schleisische Volkslieder in 1842.

3. This is the final stanza from "In the Bleak Midwinter," written by the English poet Christina Rossetti. It was published under the title "A Christmas Carol" in the January 1872 issue of *Scribner's Monthly*. In 1906, the composer Gustav Holst composed a setting of Rossetti's words (titled "Cranham") in *The English Hymnal*.

4. "Be Thou my vision, O Lord of my heart" is based on an Irish poem attributed to Dallán Forgaill (530–598). In 1905 it was translated into English by Mary Elizabeth Byrne, then revised and published by Eleanor Hull in 1912. It has been commonly sung to an Irish folk tune.

5. C. S. Lewis, *Till We Have Faces* (Geoffrey Bles, 1956).

6. Frederick Buechner, *Secrets in the Dark: A Life in Sermons* (HarperCollins, 2007).

7. Richard Rohr, *Near Occasions of Grace* (Orbis Books, 2015).

8. John Irving, *A Prayer for Owen Meany* (Knopf Canada, 2012).

9. J. R. R. Tolkien, *The Lord of the Rings* (Allen & Unwin, 1954–55).

10. Madeleine L'Engle, "The Possible Human," Madeleine L'Engle Papers, Archives of Wheaton College, Wheaton, Illinois.

11. C.S. Lewis, *Prince Caspian* (Geoffrey Bles, 1951).

12. Information about water supply in Africa is derived from the following sources: Sandy Cairncross, "Domestic Water Supply in Rural Africa," in *Rural Transformation in Tropical Africa*, ed. Douglas Rimmer (Ohio University Press, 1988); and Ann-Christin Sjolander Holland, *The Water Business: Corporations versus People* (Zed Books, 2005).

13. Jacinta is fictional. Details of her life were derived from information found in these sources: David Hemson, "Easing the burden on women? Water, cholera and poverty in South Africa," in *Poverty and Water: Explorations of the Reciprocal Relationship*, ed. David Hemson, Kassim Kulindwa, Haakon Lein, and Adolfo Mascarenhas (Zed Books, 2008); and Gilbert F. White, David J. Bradley, and Anne U. White, *Drawers of Water: Domestic Water Use in East Africa* (The University of Chicago Press, 1972).

# About the Author

**LORI VOS** grew up in the beautiful Niagara region on the shore of Lake Ontario before moving across the lake to Kingston, where she now lives with her husband, Ray. She teaches academic writing at Queen's University and writes in several genres: children's literature, short fiction, poetry, and creative non-fiction.

# SHANTI ARTS

## NATURE ▪ ART ▪ SPIRIT

Please visit us online
to browse our entire book
catalog, including poetry
collections and fiction, books
on travel, nature, healing, art,
photography, and more.

Also take a look at our highly
regarded art and literary journal,
*Still Point Arts Quarterly*, which
may be downloaded for free.

WWW.SHANTIARTS.COM

CPSIA information can be obtained
at www.ICGtesting.com
Printed in the USA
LVHW032027261022
731646LV00025B/464